THE
COVENANT STORY
OF THE
BIBLE

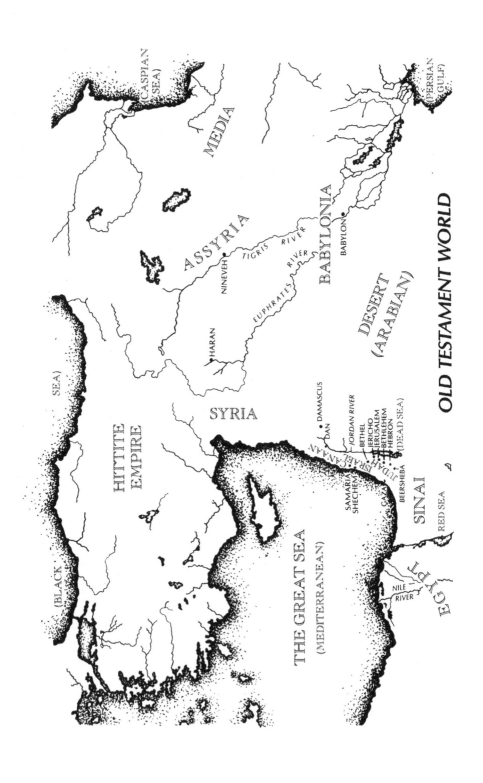

OLD TESTAMENT WORLD

THE
COVENANT STORY
OF THE
BIBLE

Alexander Campbell

WIPF & STOCK · Eugene, Oregon

Wipf and Stock Publishers
199 W 8th Ave, Suite 3
Eugene, OR 97401

The Covenant Story of the Bible
By Campbell, Alexander
Copyright©1986 Pilgrim Press
ISBN 13: 978-1-60608-862-3
Publication date 6/5/2009
Previously published by Pilgrim Press, 1986

**To my wife, Pat,
Partner in Covenant**

CONTENTS

PART TWO—THE NEW COVENANT

ILLUSTRATIONS

8

FOREWORD

When a former student brings forth a notable literary offspring, a teacher has the unique satisfaction that comes to one who is a grandparent. One's delight with the continuity of the family lineage is matched only by the joyful acknowledgment that one's spiritual children show an increasing measure of creative insight and disciplined devotion.

The larger family lineage to which Alexander Campbell and I belong is the covenant theology that has played such a prominent role in the heritage of the United Church of Christ. When my book *Invitation to Theology* was first being offered as a lay course in theology for parents and teachers, "Alex" vowed that he would try to prepare a corresponding study book for the young people who participate in confirmation and church membership classes. This is why I am so pleased to be asked to celebrate its birth!

I wish to commend Pastor Campbell for having identified with such clarity and having retold with such warmth and simplicity the covenant theme that runs through the story of the Bible. Along with the efforts of specially trained scholars who give us the best possible translation of the earliest biblical manuscripts and who tell us what the original authors meant to say, there is need for other teachers to help us to find the way to read the Bible with sufficient insight and self-understanding that we can discern what God means for us to be and to do as we become involved in the story of God's mighty acts.

In *The Covenant Story of the Bible* the author unfolds the biblical drama of covenant-making by God, of covenant-breaking by God's unfaithful people, and of covenant-renewal by God in and through Jesus the Christ. I am confident that the young people of the churches who read it will say, "This is the story of *our* lives."

Professor Emeritus   ALLEN O. MILLER
Eden Theological Seminary
Webster Groves, Missouri

ACKNOWLEDGMENTS

This book is the product of a struggle to answer the question: How do I adequately communicate the story of the Bible to those who are beginning the journey of biblical understanding? Conversations with Allen O. Miller, professor of systematic theology emeritus at Eden Theological Seminary, greatly assisted me in finding an answer to that question. As a former student of Dr. Miller I feel deeply indebted to him, not only for insight into the crucial significance of the covenant for the biblical drama, but also for the encouragement he gave me as I prepared this book.

I should like to express my gratitude to members of youth and adult classes who have been the sounding board for much of the material presented in this book. I owe a debt of gratitude to the late Allen Wehrli, professor of Old Testament at Eden Seminary, who communicated to me and to hundreds like me his deep appreciation of the Bible. The influence of this twentieth-century biblical storyteller par excellence will be readily recognized in more than one place by those who have feasted in his classes. A word of thanks is also due Robert Koenig, Lionel Whiston, the late Dr. Harold Pflug, and Dorothea Pflug.

A special word of appreciation goes to my typist, Lorraine Holzborn, who had to decipher a self-taught brand of typing. The word to my children, Debbie and Beth Ann, is one of petition for forgiveness for all the times I "did not have time." My final word is one of loving gratitude to my wife, Pat, who found out, firsthand, what it means to be a manuscript widow. In ways innumerable, hers was the hand behind the hand.

Avon Lake United Church of Christ   ALEXANDER CAMPBELL
Avon Lake, Ohio

A WORD TO TEACHERS

This is a book about the Bible. In that respect it is not different from hundreds of others, but I am here trying to accomplish what to my knowledge is not being otherwise attempted. The purpose of the book is threefold:

1. It seeks to bring the insights of biblical scholarship to young people and adults in a way that will be both understandable and enjoyable. It is my hope that this book will lead many to an intensive and intelligent study of the Bible. I draw on the insights of many scholars. The critical reader will recognize, however, that where there are differences of opinion among scholars, one must set forth what seems to be the most logical interpretation.

2. It seeks to portray the Bible as the great drama that it really is. Far too long we have seen the Bible subjected to unmerciful dissection by teachers, preachers, and parents. A story has been taken out of context here, a homiletical truth snatched from there, or a needed illustration conscripted from elsewhere. It is time we rescued the Bible from such fragmentation and looked at the whole story: the story of the saving grace of God in history. This story winds through the history of a nation involving patriarchs and kings, prophets and apostles, but most especially Jesus the Christ. The dividing of the biblical story into acts and scenes is carried out purposely in this book to emphasize that the Bible is a great drama played on the living stage of history.

3. It seeks to show that the meaning and story of the Bible can best be unlocked by means of a special key: the covenant. Events of Israel's history were judged in terms of the covenant God had made with Israel at Sinai. Writers of the Bible had the covenant as an ever-present yardstick. The very fact that the two divisions of our Bible are called the Old Testament (Old Covenant) and New Testament (New Covenant) indicates the importance of the idea. As one reads the Bible, one sees the covenant idea to be the golden cord that winds through the Bible's pages from beginning to end. Without some understanding of its central place in the history of Israel, one's appreciation of the Bible must certainly suffer.

This book is not meant to be an end in itself. Rather, its purpose is to point persons to the Bible. It seeks to serve as a guide to help persons to

11

find their way more intelligently through the Bible and to whet their appetite for more thorough biblical investigation. Biblical references have been included to encourage persons to read the Bible.

If the readers come to see the story of the Bible for the unique covenant drama that it is—the unfolding relationship of blessing and faithfulness between God and a people—and begin to identify themselves as actors within that drama, this book will be justified.

CHRONOLOGICAL TABLE

DATES	EVENTS AND PERSONS	BIBLE	DRAMA
B.C.	Creation	Genesis 1—2	
	Adam and Eve	Genesis 2—3	
	Cain and Abel	Genesis 4	PROLOGUE
	The flood	Genesis 6—9	
	Tower of Babel	Genesis 11	
1750	Migration to Canaan	Genesis 12	
	Abraham, Isaac, Jacob	Genesis 12—36	
	Joseph	Genesis 37—50	
1700–1600	Hebrews enter Egypt		Act I
1290	Exodus	Exodus	
	Call to Moses	Exodus 3—4	GOD
	The Passover	Exodus 11—13	
	Red Sea deliverance	Exodus 14	MAKES
	Ten commandments	Exodus 20	
	Covenant ceremony	Exodus 24	A
	Conquest of Canaan	Joshua	COVENANT
	Joshua		
1250	Fall of Jericho	Joshua 6	
1200–1020	Period of the Judges	Judges	
	Deborah	Judges 4—5	
	Gideon	Judges 6—8	
	Samson	Judges 14—16	
	The Kingdom of Israel		
1020–1000	Saul, first king	1 Samuel 8—15	
1000–961	David, second king	1 Samuel 16— 2 Samuel	
961–922	Solomon, third king	1 Kings 1—11	
922	Kingdom divides	1 Kings 12	
	Judah (Southern Kingdom)		
	Israel (Northern Kingdom)		

DATES	EVENTS AND PERSONS		BIBLE	DRAMA
B.C.	**Judah**	**Israel**		Act II
922–915	Rehoboam		1 Kings 12—14	
922–901		Jeroboam	1 Kings 12—14	
913–873	Asa		1 Kings 15	ISRAEL
873–849	Jehoshaphat		1 Kings 22	
869–850		Ahab	1 Kings 16—22	IS
		Elijah		
		Micaiah		
		Elisha	2 Kings 2—13	UNFAITHFUL
842–815		Jehu	2 Kings 9—10	
837–800	Joash		2 Kings 11—12	
800–783	Amaziah		2 Kings 14	
786–746		Jeroboam II	2 Kings 14	
750		Amos	Amos	
745		Hosea	Hosea	
783–742	Azariah (known also as Uzziah)		2 Kings 15	
742–735	Jotham	Minor Kings	2 Kings 15—17	
742–700	Isaiah		Isaiah 1—39	
	Micah		Micah	
722		Israel falls to Assyrians (End of Northern Kingdom)	2 Kings 17	
	Judah			
715–687	Hezekiah		2 Kings 18—20	
687–642	Manasseh		2 Kings 21	
640–609	Josiah (Deuteronomic Reform)		2 Kings 22—23	
628–587	Jeremiah		Jeremiah	
	Minor Kings		2 Kings 23—24	
598–571	Ezekiel		Ezekiel	
587	Judah falls to Babylonians (End of Southern Kingdom)		2 Kings 24—25	
587–538	Period of exile			
540	Second Isaiah		Isaiah 40—55	

DATES	EVENTS AND PERSONS	BIBLE	DRAMA
B.C.			
538	Return of exiles		
520–515	Rebuilding of the temple Zerubbabel	Ezra	
445–433	Rebuilding of walls of Jerusalem Nehemiah	Nehemiah	
c.442	The Law enforced Ezra		
400–167	Jews under Persian, Greek, Egyptian, and Syrian domination		
167	Maccabean revolt Judas Maccabaeus		
166–63	Jews enjoy nominal freedom		
63	Pompey captures Jerusalem; beginning of Roman domination		
6	Birth of Jesus	The	Act III
A.D.			
27–29	Baptism of Jesus	Four	NEW
29–33	Ministry of Jesus		COVENANT
30–33	Crucifixion and resurrection of Jesus Christ	Gospels	IN JESUS CHRIST
30–33	Beginning of the Christian church	Acts 2	Act IV
35	Conversion of Paul	Acts 9	LIFE
35–64	Paul's missionary journeys	Acts Pauline Letters	OF THE CHRISTIAN
64	Death of Paul		CHURCH
64 to the present	The spread of the Christian church		
	The kingdom of God and eternal life	1 Corinthians 15 Revelation	EPILOGUE

WHAT IS THE BIBLE?

The Bible contains all sorts of literature: stories, legends, hero tales, myths, poems, songs. An artist uses many colors and blends of colors to put a picture on canvas; and through that picture tells a story.

God is an artist too. God takes many people and many events and many ideas. God takes the good in people and the evil. Thousands of years of history are but a day. God takes Divine love for people and their trust or their doubt. All this and much more God takes and blends into one great masterpiece that we call the Bible. God's masterpiece is divided into two parts: the Old Testament and the New Testament.

When we use the word testament, realizing that it means covenant, we are coming close to the central theme of the story that God tells us in the Bible. The Old Testament, or Old Covenant, is the story of how God made a promise to a particular people to be with them and bless them all their days. They, in turn, would worship and serve God in loving obedience. But, alas, the story of the Old Covenant is also the story of how God's people, time and again, refused "to serve the Lord," suffered under an inevitable judgment, and failed to fulfill God's purpose.

What then, is the story of the New Testament, the New Covenant? It is the story of how God sent Jesus to change and win the hearts of people. All who really trusted in God as revealed in and through Jesus would know themselves to be God's children. Jesus' death on a cross was the final great sacrificial act which renewed the relationship of love and trust between God and all people. The resurrection of Jesus was the sign and seal that this covenant relationship between God and the people would endure through all eternity.

THE BIBLE AS A GREAT DRAMA

The Old Testament (Old Covenant) and the New Testament (New Covenant) contain God's plan to save a people and bring them into that kind of relationship that a loving parent has with a trusting child. Here we see that the Bible is actually a great drama, with one main plot: the salvation of humankind. The major actor is God. The minor actors are the people of the Bible. The scene is set in the ancient world of the Middle East, centering in Palestine. The time is about 1800 B.C. to A.D. 150. To have a

17

drama the stage must first be set. In the Bible this setting of the stage or prologue (first word) goes back beyond recorded history, back to creation. One of the most effective ways to speak of such a time is through the language of religious symbolism. Thus the story of creation and the fall, and indeed the first eleven chapters of Genesis, may be referred to as the prologue of the biblical drama. This is followed by the first act of the drama, the first scene of which deals with God's call to Abraham. The general outline of the biblical drama to be followed in this book is as follows:

PROLOGUE: The writers of the Bible set the scene for us: creation, the fall, Cain & Abel, the flood, Tower of Babel. (Genesis 1—11)

ACT I: God prepares a people for a covenant and finally brings them into a covenant relationship. (Abraham to David—the most important scene here is the one about the exodus and Moses)

ACT II: The people do not keep their part of the covenant and suffer under God's judgment. (Solomon to exile and postexilic period)

ACT III: God comes in Jesus to bring people into a new relationship of love and trust with their God. (The four Gospels)

ACT IV: The birth and spread of the Christian church is guided by the Holy Spirit. (Acts of the Apostles, letters of Paul)

EPILOGUE: A look ahead to the kingdom of God and eternal life. (1 Corinthians 15; Book of Revelation)

THE IMPORTANCE OF THE COVENANT

As we have noted above, the word covenant refers to that holy relationship of love and trust between God and God's people. In the covenant relationship we have a key that can unlock the Bible story for us, swinging open the door to a greater and clearer understanding of it.

The covenant relationship between God and the people might be compared on the human side to the relationship between a wife and a husband. Each is bound to the other in what is meant to be an unbreakable bond. In a similar way, Israel was bound to "the Lord" by such a bond. To what extent did the bond, this covenant relationship between God and Israel, influence the writers of the Bible story?

As we read the first chapter of Genesis, noting one of the accounts of how God created the world and man and woman and how God blessed them, we realize this is that good relationship that God would have with all persons.

As we follow the story of the flood and lift our eyes to a rainbow, we see God's promise to a people to be with them.

As we listen to the call of God as it comes to Abraham, we discover in the patriarch's acceptance of this call the beginning of the working out of the great covenant plan.

As we feel into the situation of Joseph whose brothers throw him into a deep well, we begin to suspect that through this lowly outcast in the mud, God is preparing better things for this people.

As we journey with Moses when the thunderings of Sinai fill the desert air, we feel the awesomeness of the moment as God and Israel covenant together.

The more we read, the clearer it becomes that one event after another unfolds itself around the covenant. In varying degree, the biblical writers were under its influence and so wrote accordingly. In brief, one might say that the story of the Bible contains the story of the covenant as it is made, broken, and remade again and again. The reason for tracing the path of this covenant story through the Bible is that, in the words of the hymn "In Christ There Is No East or West," it is the "golden cord close binding all mankind"—close binding all persons to God and to one another.

When Did the Covenant Begin?

The covenant between God and a particular people began with the exodus, the escape of the Israelites under Moses from slavery in Egypt. The exodus is the key event of the entire Old Testament, the pivotal event around which all else turns.

What did the exodus mean to the Hebrew people? It had a religious meaning. It meant that God had chosen them as a special people. God would lead, guide, and bless them. They, in turn, would be faithful to God. This was the covenant. When Israel's historians, who lived many years later, recorded the history of their nation, they did so with the exodus and the covenant centrally in mind. What happened in the life of Israel prior to the exodus and the covenant was seen by them as preparing for this high moment in their history. What occurred in the life of Israel after the exodus was interpreted by them in terms of the keeping or the breaking of the covenant. It is well to keep this in mind when reading the Bible.

The Old Testament is constantly interpreted in the light of the great event of Israel's deliverance and the covenant made between God and this people. The full importance and the meaning of the event are treated in Scene 2 of Act I.

First, however, we must look at the Prologue which sets the stage in this presentation of the biblical drama for the great story of the exodus. As we read the creation accounts and the other stories taken from Genesis, we should remember one central fact. These stories were recorded by persons who lived after the exodus and who thus knew the importance of the exodus and the covenant in the life of their people. In setting down the stories, it was their aim to show how God was quietly preparing a people for a particular role on the stage of history.

We know also that they took the traditions of Israel's history that had been passed on by word of mouth from parent to child for generations and put these traditions into written form. Sometimes they made changes in the traditional stories in order to help more people understand them. Scholars who have spent their lives studying the Bible tell us that from Genesis to 2 Kings we can find four main traditions. These traditions and the symbols that stand for them are as follows:

Tradition	Point of View
J	This tradition represents the point of view of Judah, the Southern Kingdom. God is always referred to as *Yahweh*, the Lord. (A Hebrew *Y* is equivalent to our letter *J*.)
E	This tradition represents the point of view of Israel, the Northern Kingdom. God is referred to as *Elohim*, a term for deity used until the time of Moses.
D	This tradition represents the point of view found in the book of *Deuteronomy* and from this book through 2 Kings, where the concern is for the covenant between God and Israel.
P	This tradition represents the point of view of the *Priestly* element in Israel's history. The major concern of this tradition is for worship, law, and religious institutions.

It is helpful to have some knowledge of different points of view of these various biblical traditions. From time to time references will be made to them in our story by the use of their symbols: J, E, D, and P. But now let us trace the covenant story, beginning with Genesis 1:1, "In the beginning. . . ."

GOD CREATES; HUMANKIND BREAKS THE RELATIONSHIP OF LOVE AND TRUST

GOD CREATES

Somewhere, sometime, in the dim mysterious past a father told his children about the beginning of all created things. He was a man whose soul was filled with awe. He believed in a Person greater than himself, a Power far mightier than anyone or anything he knew. He looked about at the created world: at earth beneath his feet, the water of a brook nearby, the trees laden with their fruits, the plants yielding their produce. He turned his head toward heaven and beheld the eternal sun that gave him and his family warmth and light and that somehow helped all things to grow. At night he scanned the heavens and marveled at the stars beyond his ability to count. He puzzled over the greatest night light of them all, the moon. Why did they see it sometimes and at other times not at all? Why did it change its shape?

He looked at the cattle grazing on the land. He remembered the beast that he and a party of hunters had just tracked down. Then he looked at his family, and at himself. And because he was something of a philosopher—that is, a man who wondered why these things came to be and for what purpose—he thought hard and long about everything on which he looked. Then one day his son or daughter began asking him many questions.

"Where did the trees come from? How did I get here? Who put the moon up there? Why does the sun shine? Why does a cow have four legs?" And so it went.

TWO STORIES OF CREATION

We do not know all the different answers given by countless parents to their offspring. Yet we can be sure there were many, and each answer was, in effect, a little story of creation. Perhaps the story of creation we find in Genesis 2:4b-25 resembles one of these answers to the question of how it

21

all began. The story comes from an early period in Israel's history, specifically out of the J tradition. It is not a scientific answer. It was never meant to be. It is a product of religious faith, and must be understood in that light. It is the telling of religious truth by the use of symbolic language.

Another story of creation, with which you may be more familiar, is that found in the first chapter of Genesis. It was written by an author who comes out of the P tradition. It is a more recent version than that in the second chapter of Genesis, having been written about the sixth century B.C. Men and women of faith believe that it is still one of the most inspiring answers ever given to the question: "How did it all begin?"

How did it begin? It began with God. Before all created things, there was God. Before there was any world at all, and long before anything or anyone ever moved on all the face of the earth, there was God.

"In the beginning God created the heavens and the earth."

And God created the earth in just the way God wanted to make it.

It was to be made up of day and night.

It was to be surrounded by the starry expanse of the heavens.

It was to have dry land and great seas and rivers.

It was to produce growing things, such as trees, plants, grass and flowers.

It was to receive the warmth and light of the great sun during the day and the light of the moon at night. Above it were to be myriads of stars.

It was to swarm with living creatures, such as birds and fish.

It was to give birth to living creatures, such as cattle and beasts and all kinds of creeping things.

And it was so.

And God saw that it was good.

But God's world was not yet complete. God wanted to put something of the Divine Self into it. So God made human beings, male and female. And this is the wonder of it. God made them in the divine image, after God's own spiritual likeness. Now God could have fellowship with them and they could talk with God. In addition, God gave into their keeping everything else that was made on all the face of the earth.

"Be fruitful and multiply" said God, "and fill the earth and subdue it; and have dominion over the fish of the sea and over the birds of the air and over every living thing that moves upon the earth."

So, God, the Creator, made man and woman to live in the world as trusting stewards of all that God had given them. And all that God made was very good.

Such is the inspiring story of creation as it meets us in the opening chapter of Genesis. However, there were those Hebrew sages who were well aware that people did not always live according to God's will. On the contrary, they all too often did evil things not intended by God. How could this be explained?

HUMANKIND DISOBEYS

The J tradition gives us a story to explain people's wrong ways of acting: the story of Adam and Eve in the Garden of Eden. In order to understand this story, we should become acquainted with its symbolic language:

Garden of Eden—means a place of fellowship with God.
Adam—comes from a Hebrew word meaning "man" in the sense of all humankind.
Eve—means life, the occasion for temptation.
Serpent—represents the human desire to become like God, to disobey God's will.
Tree of the knowledge of good and evil—means the power that belongs only to God.

God had created humankind with the freedom to obey God or to disobey. Only such freedom made real life possible. But having such freedom opened the door to temptation.

God had given Adam orders to stay away from the tree of knowledge. Adam was to act as a trusting son obeying the command of his father. But the serpent, humankind's evil desiring, was strong. Through Eve—that is, life with its temptations—the serpent enticed Adam to eat of the fruit of the forbidden tree. By choice, Adam ate of the fruit and so disobeyed God. This showed that Adam did not trust in God or in God's holy will. It also showed that Adam wanted to put self instead of God at the center of life.

THE CONSEQUENCES OF DISOBEDIENCE

Immediately the man and the woman became ashamed of their rebellion and tried to hide from God. But God came seeking them to judge them for the evil thing they had done. The consequence of their sinful deed was that they were thrown out of the garden. They had, by their own actions, rejected a trusting fellowship with God. What happens when persons live apart from God is portrayed for us in three key stories, which we find in the first eleven chapters of Genesis: the story of Cain and Abel (Genesis 4:1-9); the story of the flood (Genesis 6—9); and the story of the Tower of Babel (Genesis 11:1-9).

The story of Cain is from the J tradition. Whether this is a tale taken from a tradition long since obscured or whether it is an original story, no one can say. It really does not matter, for the point remains: When people are at odds with God they will be at odds with their brothers and sisters also. Or, to put it another way, when we see a person who is angry with, and jealous of, another person in the way that Cain was with Abel, we see one who is, at that moment, not very close to God.

Cain is a symbol of a person who is so cut off from God and God's will that he can commit the deed of murdering his own brother in cold blood. And, when God comes around to ask where Abel is, Cain simply retorts: "I do not know; am I my brother's keeper?"

The writings of the J tradition and the P tradition are brought together by an editor, whom we shall call RP, to make up the story of the flood as we have it in Genesis 6—9. How are we to understand this story? Was there really a great flood that covered the whole face of the earth? Did a boat, called the ark, really sail around and around for about five months, filled with all kinds of animals and birds and a few people? Did the waters cover the highest mountains of the earth?

There are some things we should get clear. First of all, other cultures have had their own flood stories. The one with which we are most familiar comes out of Babylonia. Many of the details of that story are very similar to the one we find in Genesis. This would suggest that here was a story well known to the peoples of the ancient Semitic world and especially to the people of Palestine. The story may very well have been based on a great flood that occurred in an ancient time. However, the "world" of this ancient account may have been only that of the valley of the Tigris and Euphrates Rivers, two rivers that have flooded the land around them more than once in history.

We must always remember that the "world" of ancient peoples was very much smaller than ours. It was limited to a definite area, beyond which most of the local inhabitants never ventured. These people lived in a day when the world was thought to be flat. Above this flat surface of the world, it was assumed that there was a great expanse of arching sky, called "the firmament" in Genesis 1. Surrounding all this above and below was water. Once in a while holes in the bottom of the sea and holes in the sky opened up and some of the surrounding water poured in. Unless you understand how people thought of the world long ago, you cannot make any sense of some of the things the biblical writers say; but, if you do understand, then you know what the P tradition is referring to when it says: "In the six hundredth year of Noah's life,* in the second month, on the seventeenth day of the month, on that day all the fountains of the great deep burst forth, and the windows of the heavens were opened [Gen. 7:11]."

The flood story is interesting because it helps us to see very clearly both the J tradition and the P tradition at work, and the differences between them. The J tradition refers to both clean and unclean animals (Genesis

*These fantastic ages of persons mentioned in the early Genesis chapters may have had a symbolic meaning now lost to us.

7:2), and to the flood that continued forty days (Genesis 7:12, 17). The P tradition makes no distinction between clean and unclean animals (Genesis 6:19; 7:14), and it states that the "waters prevailed upon the earth a hundred and fifty days [Gen. 7:24]."

If there were differences between them however, both J and P agreed on one thing: the reason for the flood. People had been guilty of great wrong, and this was God's means of punishing them. Let us be clear. The flood story is not to be thought of as an actual event that happened just the way the biblical writers described it. It is to be thought of as a parable by which the ancient writers sought to tell a moral or spiritual truth. The truth they were telling here is that evil does not go on and on without being recompensed in a day of judgment. Again, this is what happens when persons choose to cut themselves off from their Maker.

The story of the Tower of Babel is not the scientific answer to why the peoples of the earth speak so many different languages. The biblical story is primarily concerned with human beings and their own exalted opinion of themselves.

"Come, let us build ourselves . . . a tower with its top in the heavens" really means "Let us show God we are just as good as God is; let's bow down and worship ourselves." This is what we call the sin of pride. Pride happens when persons forget that although they have been made in God's image, they are still human creatures. When, because of their accomplishments, people no longer humble themselves before their Maker, the sin of pride has taken hold of them. But such are in for a fall. This was perhaps symbolized to an ancient Semite by a half-finished tower seen one day in the desert.

But what now of humankind's exclusion from this intimate relationship with God by their own choice? Would God leave them on their own, not caring what happened to them? Far from it. For now the biblical writers have set the stage for the great drama that is to follow. Even though humankind broke away from God, God had not deserted them. God would constantly search after them, would constantly pursue them in order to bring them back to the God who is their God. This is the plot of the biblical drama. The Old Testament is the story of a loving God acting to save humankind through a particular people, the Israelites, and for a particular purpose, that all nations might be blessed. The New Testament is the story of how God accomplished the divine purpose in Jesus Christ.

The biblical writers saw the creation and the fall and its attendant stories as the setting of the stage for this story, a story that leads up to and follows from the covenant between God and Israel. We shall begin to see the influence of the covenant idea in the time of the patriarchs.

Part One

THE
OLD
COVENANT

GOD CHOOSES ISRAEL

Scene 1.
GOD PREPARES A PEOPLE
(Abraham to Joseph)

Now the Lord said to Abram, "Go from your country and your kindred and your father's house to the land that I will show you. And I will make of you a great nation, and I will bless you, and make your name great, so that you will be a blessing. I will bless those who bless you, and him who curses you I will curse; and by you all the families of the earth shall bless themselves."

—Genesis 12:1–3

GOD CALLS ABRAHAM

Although the history of Israel as a nation really begins with the exodus, the early beginnings of Israel trace back to Abraham.* The history begins with the recorded call of God to Abraham. Abraham's point of departure was the city of Haran in northern Mesopotamia. It is from Haran that Abraham and his wife Sarah and his nephew Lot and their families—an entire tribe or clan—began the adventurous journey into an unknown and strange land. This was not a quick trip. Months, even years, may have been spent by this small Aramaean band as they traveled northwest from Haran across the Fertile Crescent and then south to a point west of the Dead Sea. Theirs was but one of many migrations taking place in the eighteenth century B.C.

If we were interested only in the cold facts of history, we should not pay much attention to this journey of a small group of wandering Aramaeans. But our interest is more than that of the objective historian, as was the concern of the biblical writers. Ours and theirs is the viewpoint of faith, the covenant faith. This is not just another migration of an insignificant

---

*Known earlier as Abram.

clan. This is the beginning of the purpose of God to make a people, a people who would be divinely blessed and who were in turn to be a blessing to all peoples. This was a call from God, a call that came to Abraham: "Go . . . and I will bless you."

ABRAHAM AND ISAAC

A clan under Abraham's leadership went to Canaan and settled there. In Abraham we see a man who had a sense of God's presence and purpose. Such a sense marked him for a special assignment. Although very much human and not without his faults, Abraham was devoted to God's will, whatever it was. An example of this devotion comes to us through a tale in Genesis from the E tradition. Abraham is called of God to offer his own son as a human sacrifice on a certain mountain. In those days human sacrifice was not unheard of as a religious practice. But to give one's son, this was almost too much. Then, too, Isaac was his only son, his heir. He was to be the carrier of the covenant promise. How could he sacrifice him? Whatever Abraham's thought, the story relates only his obedience. It was a three-day journey to the place of sacrifice. So one morning early, with a couple of servants, Abraham and his son began their trip. When they finally reached their destination, as they were walking to the top of the hill where the ritual was to be performed, Isaac asked his father what the sacrifice was.

"God will provide," replied Abraham.

Then Abraham took Isaac, bound him hand and foot upon the altar, and raised his knife to kill him. At that moment he heard God speak to him, saying: "Do not lay your hand on the lad or do anything to him; for now I know that you fear God, seeing you have not withheld your son, your only son, from me."

When God had finished speaking, Abraham saw a ram caught in the bushes. This he killed and offered as a sacrifice in place of Isaac.

Did Abraham misunderstand God's intention? Did God really intend for Abraham to sacrifice his son? Whatever the case, this story shows us Abraham's complete devotion to God. No wonder that following upon this incident we read of God's blessing Abraham and his descendants because of his faithfulness. Such was the stature of this father of the patriarchs who in more than a figurative sense was the father of a mighty nation.

Isaac and his son Jacob carried forward the blessing given to Abraham. In the case of Jacob, the blessing was carried forward in a rough-and-tumble way. We see him as a smooth-skinned schemer who gets into trouble with his brother Esau by cheating him out of his father's blessing. He runs away to stay with his uncle for fourteen years, and ends up in a hassle with him. The biblical writer even portrays Jacob as having trouble with God. Yet through it all, the blessing of the nation that is to be goes with him.

JOSEPH: FAVORITE AND SLAVE

It is, however, the story of Joseph, beloved son of Jacob, that really captures our attention next; for it is through him that the Israelite tribes, at least most of them, finally find their way into Egypt. The story as we now have it comes from the E and the J traditions.

When we are first introduced to Joseph, he appears to us as a big show-off. We do not wonder that his brothers called him "father's pet." He was. His father even made a special coat for him, and Joseph was only too ready to parade it in front of his brothers. But it was too much when he told his brothers his dreams. In one of them, he said, they were all binding sheaves of grain in a field. Suddenly his sheaf stood straight up and their sheaves all gathered around and bowed down to his. This really made his brothers angry. Who did Joseph think he was? Patiently they awaited their chance to get even. One day, that chance came. The brothers were in another part of the country watching the family sheep. Jacob wanted to know how they were getting along, so he sent Joseph to find out. As soon as Joseph reached his brothers, they grabbed him and tore off his robe and threw him in a deep well. They would have killed him if one of the older brothers had not intervened. What, then, should they do with him?

The J tradition tells us in Genesis 37:25–27, 28b that his brothers sold him to a group of passing Ishmaelite traders. The E tradition reports in Genesis 37:18, 22–23a, 24, 28a that a Midianite caravan lifted him out of the pit. In either case, the important fact is that Joseph arrived in Egypt, for this was the caravan's destination. There he was sold (in those days buying and selling slaves was commonplace) to a man named Potiphar, the captain of the pharaoh's guard.

JOSEPH: INTERPRETER AND OVERSEER

In Canaan, Jacob was deep in sorrow. He thought Joseph was dead. His brothers had dipped his coat in the blood of a goat and had invented a story that Joseph had been killed by a wild animal. But Joseph was very much alive. Although he was sent to jail on trumped-up charges, he managed to get the ear of the Egyptian pharaoh through his ability to interpret dreams. When the pharaoh's own magicians failed him, he sent for Joseph and told him his two dreams:

> Behold, in my dream I was standing on the banks of the Nile; and seven cows, fat and sleek, came up out of the Nile and fed in the reed grass; and seven other cows came up after them, poor and very gaunt

31

and thin, such as I had never seen in all the land of Egypt. And the thin and gaunt cows ate up the first seven fat cows, but when they had eaten them no one would have known that they had eaten them, for they were still as gaunt as at the beginning.

—Genesis 41:17–21

This dream was repeated with seven good ears on a stalk and seven bad ears replacing the imagery of the cows.

The dream was interpreted by Joseph to indicate that there would be seven years of good and abundant crops. This would be followed by seven bad years of famine. Joseph's advice was to begin now in the good years to store up food against the coming bad years. Joseph's reward for his dream interpretation was not long in coming. He was made chief overseer in charge of food production and storage, with power second only to that of the pharaoh. Thus Joseph prospered in Egypt. The way was then being prepared for the next part of the story.

The time of famine came upon the land. It came not just to Egypt but to the surrounding lands as well. The Egyptians' warehouses were filled to overflowing; they had more than was necessary for their own use. They were thus able to sell grain to people from other countries. Many came up to take advantage of Egypt's surplus. Among those who came were Joseph's brothers, for the famine was great in Canaan. Joseph had not seen his brothers in years. By now they may have thought him dead. What would be in Joseph's heart? They were his own flesh and blood, but they had sold him into slavery. Would he seek revenge as they had so many years ago?

Joseph was present when they came to buy grain, but his brothers did not recognize him. The number of years that had passed and his Egyptian dress could have kept them from knowing who he was. He did not sell them grain; he gave it to them. But he also demanded something. He asked that on their return trip they bring Benjamin, their youngest brother, with them. To ensure that, he kept one of the brothers, Simeon, as a hostage.

When they returned and told Jacob that the Egyptian overseer wanted to see Benjamin, their father's reaction was a violent *no!* He had lost one son whom he dearly loved and he did not want to take the chance of losing another. Finally, however, Jacob had to give in, for Simeon was still being held as a hostage and the food supply was almost gone. With considerable misgiving, he said good-bye to his older sons and Benjamin, wondering in his heart if he would ever see them again.

Once more they began the tiresome journey to Egypt. They were given a royal welcome upon their arrival, a great feast having been prepared in their honor. This mystified them. They enjoyed it, but they were more than a little suspicious. Why should an Egyptian official treat them like this?

JOSEPH: FORGIVER AND GOD'S SERVANT

Joseph was overjoyed to see his brothers, especially Benjamin. In fact, he had to excuse himself so that he could weep in private, so overcome was he. But Joseph was not yet ready to accept his brothers and to forgive them for the treachery they had committed against him. So he put them to a test.

As the brothers were preparing to leave, he ordered his servant to slip a silver cup secretly into the bag of Benjamin. After the brothers had taken their leave, Joseph sent in pursuit his servants who then accused the brothers of stealing a silver cup. Imagine the chagrin on the faces of the brothers when the cup was found in the bag of Benjamin! Now what would happen? Would their father's fears be confirmed? Would he lose Benjamin too?

Returning to the palace, they heard Joseph say, "The man in whose hand the cup was found shall be my slave." The others were free to go. Immediately Judah, one of the brothers, stepped forward. He explained to Joseph, whom he still did not recognize, that if Benjamin did not return, the shock would kill his father. And then he said, "Now therefore, let your servant, I pray you, remain instead of the lad as a slave to my lord; and let the lad go back with his brothers." Judah was willing to sacrifice his life in place of Benjamin.

This was too much for Joseph. In the face of this gesture of self-giving love, Joseph utterly broke down. He then revealed himself to his brothers by saying simply, "I am Joseph." Never was there such a reunion! In the midst of tears they embraced and kissed one another. All strife and enmity were gone. They were one family once more.

We see the hand of the covenant-inclined Hebrew author at work when Joseph says, "do not be distressed, or angry with yourselves, because you sold me here; for God sent me before you to preserve life . . . to preserve for you a remnant on earth [Gen. 45:5,7]."

A little later Joseph says to his brothers: "As for you, you meant evil against me; but God meant it for good, to bring it about that many people should be kept alive, as they are today [Gen. 50:20]." And just before his death, Joseph says: "I am about to die; but God will visit you, and bring you up out of this land to the land which he swore to Abraham, to Isaac, and to Jacob [Gen. 50:24]."

In the narrative of Joseph, as in the narratives of all the patriarchs, we see the conviction of the Hebrew writers that God was already preparing a people for a particular destiny and a particular role in history. It would be

33

some four hundred years until the event would occur that was to propel them toward that destiny. Nevertheless, it would come. And it would never be forgotten.

Scene 2.
GOD MAKES A COVENANT
(Exodus and the Moral Law)

MOSES: MEMORIES AND QUESTIONS

A bleak, dry, mountainous land interrupted here and there by scattered places of vegetation—this was the wilderness of the Sinai peninsula. Here, for about forty years, Moses lived the life of a shepherd, charged with the safety of the flock of his father-in-law Jethro. Here he married Zipporah, Jethro's daughter, and here a son was born to them. Moses seemed comfortably settled in Midian for the rest of his life.

But God had other plans for him, plans that were to place him at the very center of the covenant drama. During all the years of his life in Midian, these plans were working themselves out within him. As he spent day after day in the solitude of the wilderness as a shepherd, he had plenty of time to think and to meditate. During this time he must have had many thoughts about his people, the Israelites. These probably included thoughts of the sufferings of the Israelites in the land of Egypt and of their oppression at the hands of cruel taskmasters. Here the Egyptians forced the Israelites to make bricks for the mammoth building projects of the pharaohs. Once the Israelites had been respected, or at least tolerated, by the Egyptians, but later they were treated as mere slaves. As Moses thought about his people, he did not feel that there was any reason to expect that their lot was easier than when he last saw them forty years earlier.

There were other thoughts too. Moses thought of his providential escape from death as a child. This was at a time when the pharaoh had ordered all male Hebrew children killed. His mother had ingeniously saved him by floating him in a basket among the reeds, so that the daughter of the pharaoh would find him. She did find him and unwittingly hired Moses' own mother to nurse him until he was older; then he was reared in the courts of the pharaoh. So, Moses was wise in the ways of the Hebrews and wise in the ways of the Egyptians.

He must have thought also of how he had killed an Egyptian taskmaster who was beating a Hebrew. This was the cause of his having left Egypt years ago.

These were some of the thoughts that must have come to Moses again

34

and again. And with the thoughts came questions. Why was he saved as a child and educated so well? What of the Hebrews who groaned in slavery in Egypt? Who would save them? How could he help? Could it be that somewhere in this picture there was a place for him?

A BUSH AND A CALL

These thoughts were brought to a climax on a certain day under the impact of an unusual experience. According to the J tradition, Moses saw a bush that looked as if it were aflame, but it did not burn up.

How was this possible? We do not know. Our explanations are only theories. We do not know for sure. We must remember that for the writers of these biblical stories, there was simply no problem. Sometimes they embellished an already exaggerated tale or traditional story, if by doing so they could better make their point. Sometimes they gave us the tradition just as it came to them. They were not as concerned about the operation of physical laws as we are today. Why should not a bush burn and not be consumed if God willed it? And so it was with many other events.

When all has been said, we are still confronted with a mystery; namely, that in a certain way and at a certain time, God spoke, called, and acted to save a people. We must remember as we read the biblical account that the Bible is filled with all kinds of carriers of spiritual truth: legends, myths, parables, hero tales, poems, songs, and narratives. We must be as wise as humanly possible to discern the facts, historical and spiritual.

But we must not get bogged down in our adventure each time we come across something we do not completely understand. If we do, we will face the danger of missing the central action of the biblical drama. Our concern is to follow the relationship between God and a particular people as the biblical writers portray it for us. It is to trace the great plot of the biblical drama: how God was acting to save all people. To this plot we now return in order to witness its further unfolding as God confronts Moses in the wilderness.

When Moses approached the burning bush, God said:

> I have seen the affliction of my people who are in Egypt, and have heard their cry because of their taskmasters; I know their sufferings, and I have come down to deliver them out of the hand of the Egyptians, and to bring them up out of that land to a good and broad land, a land flowing with milk and honey.
>
> —Exodus 3:7–8

God chose Moses for a special task. To him was given the gigantic undertaking of leading the Hebrews out of Egypt. What was Moses' reaction to this command from God? Did he accept it eagerly? Quite the contrary. Scripture records that he offered four excuses why he should not

35

be the one so chosen. Each time God refused to accept his excuse. Of the four excuses offered, the answer to the second given to us by the E tradition is the most illuminating. Moses said if he went to lead the people, they would ask him the name of the God who sent him. God replied: "Say this to the people of Israel, 'I AM has sent me to you. . . . The Lord, the God of your fathers, the God of Abraham, the God of Isaac, and the God of Jacob, has sent me to you [Exod. 3:14–15].'"

In other words, the God who caused all things to be, who made everything, the God of their ancestors—this is the God whose bidding Moses was to do. This is the first time the E tradition uses the name Yahweh as the name of the Lord. Confronted by the will of the Almighty, Moses finally gave in and returned to Egypt to lead his people.

MOSES CONFRONTS PHARAOH

Moses went before the pharaoh and demanded that the Hebrews be allowed to leave Egypt. Pharaoh not only laughed in his face but he made the work load for the Hebrews even worse. It is not surprising that the Israelites growled against Moses about their condition.

Moses, however, was persistent. After counsel with God, he went back to see the pharaoh time and again. After each visit, a plague would come upon the land. Yet after each plague was over, the pharaoh's heart was hardened and he would not let the people go.

The death of the firstborn was the plague that changed the pharaoh's mind. The biblical account relates that none of the Hebrew families was touched because the blood of the sacrificial lamb had been spread on their doorposts so that the angel of death would pass over them. Not so the families of the Egyptians, where the firstborn of every household felt the touch of death.

Was this really a time of some great pestilence that swept through the ancient world, including Egypt? Is it possible that such a pestilence struck forcefully at the Egyptians, while leaving the separated Hebrew colony untouched? Again, we do not know. Whatever the case, this event was seen by the Hebrews as a direct action of God to obtain their release. And at this point the pharaoh was only too happy to let them go!

THE EXODUS

With no hesitation the Hebrews made ready and headed for the wilderness of Sinai under the leadership of Moses and his right-hand man, Aaron. They had not gone very far, however, when the pharaoh had a change of heart. Why should he let all this free labor slip right out of his hand? Quickly he summoned his charioteers and sent them out to pursue the Hebrews. In no time at all, the Egyptians caught up with the fleeing

Israelites. With the Red Sea in front of them and the pursuing Egyptians behind them, a massacre seemed imminent. At just this moment occurred that mighty act of God that the Israelites from generation to generation would never tire of telling their children. The scriptural account, weaving together the J, E, and P sources, cannot be surpassed in the telling of the event:

> Then Moses stretched out his hand over the sea; and the Lord drove the sea back by a strong east wind all night, and made the sea dry land, and the waters were divided. And the people of Israel went into the midst of the sea on dry ground, the waters being a wall to them on their right hand and on their left. The Egyptians pursued, and went in after them into the midst of the sea, all Pharaoh's horses, his chariots, and his horsemen. And in the morning watch the Lord in the pillar of fire and of cloud looked down upon the host of the Egyptians, and discomfited the host of the Egyptians, clogging their chariot wheels so that they drove heavily; and the Egyptians said, "Let us flee from before Israel; for the Lord fights for them against the Egyptians."
>
> Then the Lord said to Moses, "Stretch out your hand over the sea, that the water may come back upon the Egyptians, upon their chariots, and upon their horsemen." So Moses stretched forth his hand over the sea, and the sea returned to its wonted flow when the morning appeared; and the Egyptians fled into it, and the Lord routed the Egyptians in the midst of the sea. The waters returned and covered the chariots and the horsemen and all the host of Pharaoh that had followed them into the sea; not so much as one of them remained. But the people of Israel walked on dry ground through the sea, the waters being a wall to them on their right hand and on their left.
>
> Thus the Lord saved Israel that day from the hand of the Egyptians; and Israel saw the Egyptians dead upon the seashore. And Israel saw the great work which the Lord did against the Egyptians, and the people feared the Lord; and they believed in the Lord and in his servant Moses.
>
> —Exodus 14:21–31

WHAT THE EXODUS MEANT

Thus the Hebrews were saved on that day, a day never to be forgotten in the annals of Israelite history. This was the day and this was the event that ever after reminded Israel that God had chosen them and that they were God's special people. It was this event, the marvelous deliverance at the Red Sea, perhaps more precisely called the Sea of Reeds, that firmly forged the covenant between God and the Israelites.

The exultation felt by the Hebrews in this moment was echoed by

Miriam, the sister of Moses, in one of the most ancient of songs to be found in the Bible: "Sing to the Lord, for he has triumphed gloriously; the horse and his rider he has thrown into the sea [Exod. 15:21]."

Thus the Israelites were saved from the hand of the Egyptians. After a period of further travel, they camped at the foot of an imposing mountain called Mount Sinai (known also as Mount Horeb). Moses may have been familiar with this mountain from his shepherding days. So impressive was it, that the Hebrews associated it with the presence of God.

THE TEN COMMANDMENTS

It is in the setting of Mount Sinai that we are introduced to the ten commandments.

Did Moses give the ten commandments? If we think of them in the form that we now have them in Exodus 20, then the answer probably has to be no. They show the work of other hands and come from a later period of Israel's history. Does this mean, then, that Moses had nothing to do with the ten commandments? Again the answer is no. It is possible that Moses himself, through the guidance of God's Spirit, was responsible for the formulation of the basic decalogue (ten words) that we find in Exodus 20. In their simplest form, the ten commandments probably looked something like this originally:

> God spoke all these words: I am Yahweh, your God, who brought you forth out of the land of Egypt, out of the house of slaves.
> 1. You shall have no other gods before me.
> 2. You shall not make for me any graven image or any likeness.
> 3. You shall not invoke the name of Yahweh your God in vain.
> 4. Remember the sabbath day to keep it holy.
> 5. Honor your father and your mother.
> 6. You shall not commit murder.
> 7. You shall not commit adultery.
> 8. You shall not steal.
> 9. You shall not bear false witness against your neighbor.
> 10. You shall not covet your neighbor's house.*

The obeying of these laws represented the Israelites' way of keeping their part of the covenant. The first four demanded their absolute trust in, and their loyalty to, God. The six others demanded that they show the right kind of responsibility to one another. All together, they represented God's claim upon the Israelites. These commandments were part and parcel of the covenant relationship. In Exodus 24:3–8, the E tradition

---

*"The History of the Religion of Israel," by James Muilenburg in *The Interpreter's Bible*, vol. I, p. 303 (Nashville: Abingdon Press, 1952).

pictures for us the awesome scene of the ratifying of this covenant between God and Israel.

THE COVENANT

Moses stands before the people, who are gathered all about him. To the back of him looms Mount Sinai, symbolic to the Hebrews of the presence of God. An altar is at the foot of the mountain. The smoke of burnt offerings trails to the very top of Mount Sinai. At a given time, Moses takes half of the blood of the sacrificed oxen and throws it against the altar. Then he reads from the book of the covenant, and the people respond (Exodus 24:7): "All that the Lord has spoken we will do, and we will be obedient."

Thereupon, Moses takes the other half of the blood and throws it on the people and says (Exodus 24:8): "Behold the blood of the covenant which the Lord has made with you in accordance with all these words."

And so the covenant was made. The Lord would be their God. They would be God's people. This marked the beginning of Israel as a holy nation, a people chosen by God. Before this they had been but scattered tribes. Now they were becoming welded together in a common bond of loyalty to the God of Sinai. This bond would draw tighter and tighter until one day they would become a great nation. Their deliverance from the Egyptians would be forever regarded as the beginning of their history as a nation. The biblical writers saw the events of their early history as leading to this point. What now followed would also be interpreted in the light of the covenant. From now on, whatever Israel did would either be in loyalty to the covenant or in disregard of it. Yet whether they were loyal or not, God had chosen a people and was not going to give up on them. God would have throughout all Israel's history leaders who would remind the people of the covenant promises their ancestors had made with Yahweh. They would remind them that the covenant was not an event that happened just once at the beginning of Israel's history. It was to be renewed in every generation.

Following the Mount Sinai encampment, the people of Israel struggled in the wilderness for forty years under the leadership of Moses. One entire generation died and never saw the promised land. Moses himself only glimpsed it from a distance. During this period he ably led the people through many difficult situations and brought them to the very threshold of the promised land. Even though he did not enter into the promised land, he is revered as the deliverer from Egypt, the lawgiver, a spokesman of the covenant, and a giant among the heroes of Israel. The book of Deuteronomy says of him:

> And there has not arisen a prophet since in Israel like Moses, whom the Lord knew face to face, none like him for all the signs and the

wonders which the Lord sent him to do in the land of Egypt, to
Pharaoh and to all his servants and to all his land, and for all the
mighty power and all the great and terrible deeds which Moses
wrought in the sight of all Israel.

—Deuteronomy 34:10–12

Scene 3.
THE STRUGGLE TO WIN
(Joshua to Judges)

THE MIRACULOUS CROSSING

It was under the leadership of Joshua that the Hebrew tribes finally
entered into Canaan, the promised land. At least this was so for most of
the tribes. There seems to have been a partial penetration of Canaan from
the south by a small Hebrew band called the Judah group. And two of the
Israelite tribes, Reuben and Gad, stayed on the east side of the Jordan,
content with the territory they had won for themselves there. However,
the main Israelite force under the command of Joshua made its entrance
into Canaan just north of the Dead Sea. This historic invasion secured for
the Israelites the foothold they needed in this new land. It was, according
to the biblical account, an invasion accompanied by wondrous signs and
events.

The first formidable obstacle that lay before the Israelites was the river
Jordan. Across it they had to transport fully equipped men of war, women,
children, cattle, and all their belongings together with the ever-present
ark of the covenant. The ark of the covenant was either a rectangular
covered box or a throne carried on two wooden poles by the officially
appointed priests. It symbolized the presence of God to the Israelites.
Indeed, it more than symbolized it. In their minds, where the ark was,
there was God. So it was guarded and revered highly by all the people.

Under Joshua's command the people made their way to the river.
Before them went the priests, carrying the ark in high and stately grandeur. Then the waters of the river began to recede until the river basin
was completely dry. Immediately the people began to cross over to the
other side. When all had crossed, the priests who bore the ark also came
forth from the river. Then twelve men gathered twelve stones from the
river under Joshua's direction and made them into a large pile in the
middle of the river. This pile of stones was to serve as a monument and a
reminder for generations to come of what God had done on this day.

What caused the river to dry up? It is possible that there was a landslide
farther up the river, perhaps at a place where two rivers joined, and that
this caused the temporary stoppage of water. This has been known to
happen in the Jordan River at other times. But you may ask, "Why is it

that this event happened at that precise moment when the Israelites wanted to cross over?" That is a question that only faith can answer. Faith sees the hand of God at work in the history of a people for whom the Almighty has a plan. Such is the way the Hebrew historians interpreted these events.

The Capture of Jericho

After the Jordan River was crossed, there loomed before the Israelites another obstacle—the fortified city of Jericho, with its great walls. If the Israelites were going to establish themselves in the land, they would have to take this city. Otherwise they ran the danger of being driven back into the Jordan River. As they camped on the plains before the city, they made a formidable sight. Tales had reached the ears of Jericho's citizens of the victories that the Israelites had won on the east side of the Jordan. Then, there was the miraculous crossing of the Jordan. All this conspired to throw terror into the hearts of the people of Jericho. Add to this the strategy employed by Joshua and you have a people ripe for defeat.

The day of the attack came. On the first day all the men of war marched around the city. Behind them came the priests blowing on trumpets made of rams' horns. Following them came the ark of the Lord (signifying God's presence). After the ark came a rear guard. This procession continued for six days. No voices were heard, no angry shouting, just the constant blaring of the rams' horns. Day after day this continued. On the seventh day they marched around the city again. They marched around seven times. On the seventh time following the priests' blowing of the trumpets, the warriors let loose with a mighty shout. The wall fell down flat, and the Israelites entered the city and took it. How did they take it? The biblical account (Joshua 6:21) reports: "Then they utterly destroyed all in the city, both men and women, young and old, oxen, sheep, and asses, with the edge of the sword."

Such was the fall and destruction of Jericho. This was the victory that marked the successful entrance of the Israelites into Canaan. What made the wall fall down? Archaeological evidence indicates that an earthquake caused the walls to tumble. This natural catastrophe could have occurred at the same time as the Israelite invasion. Records indicate that the disaster to the city occurred around the year 1250 B.C. Exact dating is impossible.

A Disturbing Question

What about the wholesale slaughter of men, women, and children? How could the Israelites do such a thing if they believed God was helping them and that they were doing God's will? Did God condone such slaughter? This is a hard question, yet it needs to be answered.

We must remember that these were a very primitive people who lived

41

by a primitive moral code. There were penalties for the killing of a member of the same tribe. In this case, justice was exacted on the basis of "an eye for an eye, and a tooth for a tooth." But when it came to enemies, their code of conduct customarily knew only one rule: destroy. They did not want to become corrupted by anything or anyone that belonged to the enemy, so they destroyed everything. In their own primitive way, they believed they were doing God's will. But their understanding of God's will 1,300 years before Christ was quite different from our understanding of it 1,900 years after Christ.

THE CONQUEST OF CANAAN

The biblical narrative moves smoothly and recounts one victory after another by the forces of Joshua in what seems like a short space of time. Actually, however, the conquest of Canaan took many, many years. Indeed, there were some elements they never did wholly succeed in driving from the land or subduing. They remained a continual thorn in the flesh for the Israelites. Chief among these people were the Philistines. When the days of Joshua came to an end, however, Israel was well established in the land. The various tribes had found their particular territories where they had decided to settle. Although fighting continued for a long time, there was no serious danger that they would be driven from Canaan. In time, the Israelites began to adopt the ways and habits of the original inhabitants of the land. Formerly they were a nomadic people who wandered from place to place tending their sheep and living in tents. Now they were settling in a land on a permanent basis. They were no longer herders of sheep; they had become farmers. They were now tied to the land.

A problem arose when they related themselves too closely to the religious customs of their neighbors. The worship of Canaan was linked up with agriculture. The farmers, who wanted good crops, worshiped a Baal, one of the many local deities believed to be a god of fertility. In too many cases, Israelite farmers felt they too had to worship the local deity to insure a good harvest. Hence their worship of the one true God became corrupted, as did some of their moral practices.

THE PROMISE AT SHECHEM

What happened to the covenant? Was it forgotten? To a certain degree, it was. The generation that had been a party to that covenant at Mount Sinai had long since passed away. The generation that had won the initial battles for Canaan had also died or were very close to dying. It was against this background that Joshua called the elders and heads of Israel together at Shechem in the hills of central Canaan.

In the hearing of all these tribal chiefs, Joshua rehearsed the mighty deeds that God had performed for the people from the time of Abraham through the great deliverance from Egypt and up to that moment. He concluded his rehearsal with these stirring words:

Now therefore fear the Lord, and serve him in sincerity and in faithfulness; put away the gods which your fathers served beyond the River, and in Egypt, and serve the Lord. And if you be unwilling to serve the Lord, choose this day whom you will serve, . . . but as for me and my house, we will serve the Lord.

—Joshua 24:14–15

The people answered Joshua as one and declared (Joshua 24:24): "The Lord our God we will serve, and his voice we will obey."

So at Shechem they ratified the covenant and promised to remain faithful to the God who had led them to that very moment. Thus they ratified their allegiance to the God of Abraham, Isaac, and Jacob and the God of Moses. When his work was finished, Joshua, the son of Nun, died and was laid to rest in the hill country of Ephraim. He was, in truth, what the biblical writer declared him to be: "the servant of the Lord."

THE JUDGES

The period of Israel's history that followed the death of Joshua (1200–1020 B.C.) was a rough-and-tumble one. There was no longer any outstanding leader such as they had known before. The tribes were widely separated, scattered now throughout the land. Even though the leaders had renewed the covenant at Shechem, the tendency on the part of the people was to worship the local gods, the Baals. Thus the pure worship of God suffered, and so did the Israelites' sense of right and wrong. It was a chaotic time.

But God never gave up on this people. God raised up "judges" to lead them. They were not judges as we think of them today. For the most part, theirs was a combination of wisdom and skill in battle. They had the kind of authoritative personality that would bring the scattered tribes of Israel running when the summons was sent out for help in the name of Yahweh. In fact, this showed that to some degree the covenant did have a binding force on the Israelite tribes. For when the call for help came, a tribe felt itself morally obligated to answer that call because it was part of the covenant made between all the tribes and their God.

DEBORAH

Among the twelve judges of Israel, three stand out: Deborah, Gideon, and Samson. Deborah along with her chief of staff, Barak, achieved a great victory in the valley of the river Kishon in northern Canaan over the forces of a local prince named Sisera. When he and his charioteers tried to attack the Israelites, the flooded river rendered their chariots helpless and they

43

DIVISION OF CANAAN

MEDITERRANEAN

SEA

SIDON

TYRE

SIDONIANS

HITTITES

ARAMEANS

DAMASCUS

MT. HERMON

DAN

DAN (LAISH)

NAPHTALI

HAZOR

ASHER

MT. CARMEL

ZEBULIN

MT. TABOR

SEA OF GALILEE

MANASSEH (EAST)

ASHTAROTH

DOR

MEGIDDO

ENDOR

SHUNEM

ISSACHAR

JEZREEL

MT. GILBOA

ROMOTH

MANASSEH (WEST)

JORDAN RIVER

JABESH

SHECHEM

GAD

AMMONITES

JOPPA

SHILOH

EPHRAIM

BETHEL

GILGAL

RABBAH

DAN

AI

BENJAMIN

JERICHO

GILBEAH

ASHDOD

JERUSALEM

BETHPEOR

LIBNAH

ASHKELON

BETHLEHEM

REUBEN

LACHISH

GAZA

JUDAH

HEBRON

(DEAD

PHILISTINES

ENGEDI

SEA)

BEERSHEBA

HORMAH

MOABITES

SIMEON

DESERT

EDOMITES

were cut down and destroyed. One of the oldest songs in the Bible celebrates this victory. It is called, quite appropriately, the Song of Deborah. The middle portion of the song tells of the tribes that came together and helped in the victory, and heaps scorn on those tribes that did not help.

> Awake, awake, Deborah!
>   Awake, awake, utter a song!
> Arise, Barak, lead away your captives,
>   O son of Abinoam.
> Then down marched the remnant of the noble;
>   the people of the Lord marched down for him against
>   the mighty.
> From Ephraim they set out thither into the valley,
>   following you, Benjamin, with your kinsmen;
> from Machir marched down the commanders,
>   and from Zebulun those who bear the marshal's staff;
> the princes of Issachar came with Deborah,
>   and Issachar faithful to Barak;
>   into the valley they rushed forth at his heels.
> Among the clans of Reuben
>   there were great searchings of heart.
> Why did you tarry among the sheepfolds,
>   to hear the piping for the flocks?
> Among the clans of Reuben
>   there were great searchings of heart.
> Gilead stayed beyond the Jordan;
>   and Dan, why did he abide with the ships?
> Asher sat still at the coast of the sea,
>   settling down by his landings.
> Zebulun is a people that jeoparded their lives to the
>   death;
>   Naphtali too, on the heights of the field.
>
> The kings came, they fought;
>   then fought the kings of Canaan,
> at Taanach, by the waters of Megiddo;
>   they got no spoils of silver.
> From heaven fought the stars,
>   from their courses they fought against Sisera.
> The torrent Kishon swept them away,
>   the onrushing torrent, the torrent Kishon.
>   March on, my soul, with might!
>   —Judges 5:12-21

GIDEON

Gideon became the deliverer of the Israelites at a time when they were suffering oppression at the hands of the Midianites, an invader from the east side of the Jordan River. Even as Deborah had done, he put out a call for help throughout the land, and the men of war assembled together just below Mount Gilboa in northern Canaan. The Midianites were across the valley beneath the hill of Moreh. With a small group of three hundred picked men, Gideon threw the Midianites into utter confusion and their soldiers fled. The Israelites pursued them across the Jordan and thoroughly defeated them.

After such a great victory, the people wanted to make Gideon king over them. But Gideon would not accept. In his thinking, there was only one king of Israel, and that was the Lord. At this time in Israel's history, the idea of a human king to rule over the people was not acceptable. In his answer to the men of Israel who had proposed this, Gideon was quite emphatic (Judges 8:23): "I will not rule over you, and my son will not rule over you; the Lord will rule over you."

Did such a great victory turn the hearts of the Hebrew people to their God? Perhaps, for a time. But in the book of Judges there is a recurring refrain typified by the account of what happened after the death of Gideon:

> As soon as Gideon died, the people of Israel turned again and played the harlot after the Baals, and made Baal-berith their god. And the people of Israel did not remember the Lord their God, who had rescued them from the hand of all their enemies on every side.
> —Judges 8:33-34

SAMSON

It would seem natural that God would weary of these people who were so fickle in their allegiance. But not so. Another champion of the people arose, one on whom the Spirit of God rested mightily. This was Samson, son of Manoah. He was a hero of the Israelites against their most persistent enemy, the Philistines. For a time the Philistines constituted a real threat to parts of Judah in southern Canaan. Even if we acknowledge that legendary exaggeration has crept into the many tales surrounding the exploits of Samson, there is no denying that these tales were based on a real person whose prowess and strength were beyond that of the ordinary man. To the delight of the oppressed Judeans, their Samson was a thorn in the flesh to the Philistines. His exploits gave them reason to hold their heads high at a time when they felt the oppressor's yoke.

Samson's recorded exploits include: the burning of the grainfields of the Philistines by tying firebrands to foxes' tails and letting the foxes run loose; the slaying of over thirty men who had killed his intended bride and her father; the slaughtering with a jawbone of an ass of over a thousand men who had come to arrest him; and the pulling out of the gates of one of the Philistines' cities to mock them. The Philistines felt that somehow they had to put a stop to all this. When Samson began visiting Delilah, they saw their chance. They offered 1,100 pieces of silver if she would betray him into their hands. She agreed and began to question Samson concerning the secret of his great strength. At first he toyed with her by giving her the wrong answers. Finally when he could stand her questions no longer, he told her that his strength was in his hair, that he had never been shaved. When he fell asleep, she cut off his hair. Then she shouted, "The Philistines are upon you, Samson!" He rose to defend himself, but in his weakness he was able to do nothing. The Philistines captured him easily, put out his eyes, and chained him to a grinding mill in the prison at Gaza.

Samson was a member of a special group of Israelites known as Nazirites. One of the marks of this group was long, unshaved hair. This was the symbol of their vow to be a Nazirite. No razor must ever be used upon the head. In Samson's case, his tremendous strength was linked up directly with his long hair. As we see in this episode near the end of his life, when his hair was cut his strength left him. At first the thought that long hair means great strength might seem fanciful. But there was something more here. The hair that was unshaved was the outward symbol of his vow to God. What really mattered was the vow. As long as he kept his vow, Samson could feel that God was with him, that his strength was really given to him by God. But when the hair was cut, he undoubtedly felt that the vow was broken, that God's Spirit had left him, and that there was no longer any power left in him. What made him weak was not the loss of his hair as such. What made him weak was the lack of confidence that God was with him.

But, now, notice what happened as his hair began to grow. His strength returned. His confidence that God's Spirit was with him also returned. On a certain feast day, the Philistines were making merry before their god Dagon. Desiring added pleasure, they asked that Samson be brought out to entertain them. A boy led out the blind Samson and placed him between the two pillars on which the palace rested. The palace was filled to overflowing with Philistines. On the roof were three thousand who could not get into the palace proper. They were using the roof as a vantage point from which to look down into the courtyard. Then came the mighty and unexpected deed which no Philistine could have foreseen. Samson called on the Lord and asked for strength just one more time. With all of the might and power within him, he exerted his weight against the two pillars. Slowly they began to give, a terrible cracking was heard, and suddenly the palace crashed to the earth with a thunderous noise and fell upon the lords and upon all the people that were in it. The scripture (Judges 16:30) testifies to this deed in the following way: "So the dead whom he slew at his death were more than those whom he had slain during his life."

The death of Samson brought to a virtual close this period in Israel's life. It was a period that was one of constant turmoil and stress. The Israelite tribes were entrenched in the land, but lacked any real unity. Time after time the worship of local deities was substituted for the worship of the one true God. The various Israelite tribes were constantly being harassed from within and without by unfriendly nations. And there were even conflicts between the Israelite tribes themselves.

Yet with all this, the picture was not completely dark. At times the tribes would come together to defend some part of the land when the call went out in the name of the God of Sinai. In the various local heroes that arose, the Israelites felt that they saw the presence of God's Spirit working for them and within them. If they had, to a great degree, forgotten the Lord, their heroic men of the Spirit showed the Israelites that the Lord had not forgotten Israel.

Indeed, the Lord was with them throughout their struggles. Even then God was preparing, in faithfulness to the covenant, to make them a great nation.

Scene 4.
HOW A KINGDOM WAS STARTED
(Samuel to Saul)

SAMUEL: PROPHET-JUDGE

Samuel was a link in the history of the Israelites. He arose at a time when some of the tribes would rally together now and then to do battle in the name of the Lord, though still as separate tribes. Each pursued its own life, each had its own communal arrangements, and each had its own particular places of worship. Except in grave emergencies, the tribes had little or no sense of responsibility toward one another. In a word, they were disunited.

By the time of Samuel, however, there were growing indications that such disunity was regarded as unsatisfactory. As separate tribes, the peoples were much more at the mercy of invaders. If they were united, they would be better able to repel hostile attacks. With a king who would rule over them and lead them, they could become a more formidable military power and perhaps a great nation.

In order to bring unity out of disunity and in order to replace an old order of things with a new, Samuel was the man of the hour to whom the people turned. Samuel stands in the unique position of being regarded as both judge and prophet. As judge, he stands last in the long line of distinguished persons who decided many difficult questions for the people and who led them into battle and gave them victory. As prophet, he stands as an early forerunner of the "spokesmen for God" who appeared later in Israel. The people looked to him as one to whom the Lord spoke. Thus, in this time of great national change, Samuel stands out as an invincible personality and as a rallying point for all Israel.

The concern to have a king was an undercurrent in the thinking of the Israelites for some time. The actual spoken demand for such a ruler was not voiced until Samuel was quite old. In his lifetime, Samuel had been an able judge and leader for them. He had a rather small circuit to travel between Bethel, Gilgal, and Mizpah in central Palestine. To these various places, however, came people from all the tribes because these were centers for religious shrines. It is not strange, therefore, that Samuel's name should be known throughout Israel. Under his leadership, a victory was won over the Philistines. This seems to have stopped their raiding for a time. Yet more trouble came when Samuel was too old to direct all the affairs of Israel by himself, and so he parceled out responsibilities to his sons. They turned out to be incompetent, more anxious for money than for justice.

The Demand for a King

In the face of the unscrupulous leadership provided by his sons and with the underlying desire to be a stronger, more unified nation, the leaders of Israel gathered together at Ramah, the home of Samuel, and asked that a king be appointed to govern their nation. Samuel was not at all sure that this was a good idea. Through many generations, God only had been their king. Leaders such as Samuel himself sought to interpret the will of God to the people. Why, now, should the people ask for an earthly king? Furthermore, did the people not realize what would happen if they had a king? He would take their sons and conscript them for an army whether they liked it or not. He would take their daughters and impress them into service. He would take the best of the fields and orchards and vineyards. The word of the king would be law, and they would be no better than slaves. Samuel painted a dark picture before the elders of Israel in an attempt to dissuade them.

But the people were insistent. Finally, after bringing the matter before God, Samuel was convinced that their demand must be met. In 1 Samuel there are two stories—an earlier account and a later one—that describe how Samuel met this demand and how Israel obtained its first king.

Saul and the Donkeys

The following story from 1 Samuel 9:1—10:16 is the older account. The story begins with a young man named Saul. He was tall and handsome, and his father was wealthy. One day his father asked Saul to take a servant and go out in search of some of their donkeys that had disappeared. Saul and the servant went from one region to another without success. The donkeys seemed to have vanished into thin air. Further search seemed hopeless. Then Saul's servant came up with an idea. There was a man in a nearby town who was supposed to be a prophet. Perhaps he could help them find the donkeys. Saul thought this was a good idea and they went to find him. The prophet turned out to be none other than Samuel. God had revealed to Samuel the preceding day that there would come a man from the land of Benjamin, a man whom he was to anoint as the one chosen to become king over the people. When Saul came into the city, Samuel knew as soon as he saw him that this must be the man about whom God had spoken. Samuel assured him first of all that the donkeys had been found. Then he prepared a choice meal for him and made a place for him to sleep on the roof of his house.

The next morning, as Saul and his servant were getting ready to leave, Samuel told the handsome Benjaminite to send his servant on before him. When they were alone, Samuel took a small vial of oil and poured it over Saul's head, saying: "Has not the Lord anointed you to be prince over his people Israel? And you shall reign over the people of the Lord and you will save them from the hand of their enemies round about [1 Sam. 10:1]."

After the secret ceremony was over, Samuel sent the king-to-be on his way. The first one to greet Saul when he returned home was his uncle. The uncle wanted to know where in the world he had been so long. Saul then told him about his fruitless search for the donkeys and how they had finally gone to ask help of Samuel, the prophet of Ramah. Saul's uncle, out of curiosity, wondered what the great man had said to Saul. "Oh," replied Saul, "he told us that the donkeys had been found." What a reply from one who had just been anointed to be the first king of Israel!

How Saul Became King

This early story of how Saul became king continues with a battle involving the town of Jabesh-gilead in the territory of Gilead. Nahash, the Ammonite, had completely surrounded the city and defeat seemed imminent. It was then that the people of the town made a strange request of their enemies. They wanted seven days to go among the tribes of Israel to try to get help. What a foolish request! Why should the Ammonites allow such a thing and thereby risk defeat? Yet that is just what they did. So convinced were they that Israel was hopelessly disunited and that Jabesh-gilead could not possibly receive any help, that they were willing to let messengers go out and scour the countryside while they sat back and laughed. In most situations, their laughter would have been justified. This time, however, they were in for a rude awakening.

While plowing his field with his oxen, news of the siege of Jabesh-gilead came to Saul. When he heard it, the Spirit of God came upon him mightily. He took a yoke of oxen, cut it into twelve pieces, and sent one piece to each of the tribes of Israel with this warning (1 Samuel 11:7a): "Whoever does not come out after Saul and Samuel, so shall it be done to his oxen!"

Did Saul's words have an effect? The scripture (1 Samuel 11:7b) relates: "Then the dread of the Lord fell upon the people, and they came out as one man."

A total of 330,000 Israelites assembled together. The Ammonites surrounding the town of Jabesh-gilead were thoroughly overwhelmed. The victory complete, Samuel summoned the people to Gilgal and there in festive ceremony publicly proclaimed Saul king over Israel.

Another writer, whose stories in 1 Samuel come from a later time, gives a different version of Saul's being chosen king. In 1 Samuel 10:17–27, he pictures a scene for us in which all the tribes of Israel come forward one by one until one tribe is chosen, the tribe of Benjamin. From this tribe is chosen the family of the Matrites, and finally from this family Saul himself is chosen. Saul, however, is nowhere to be found. After some searching, his elders find him hiding among the baggage. What an auspicious beginning for kingship! It was small wonder that some of the people were skeptical. But as he stood there, head and shoulders above everyone else, the people sensed authority and shouted, "Long live the king!"

This same writer portrays for us another scene in which Samuel, before he goes into retirement, addresses the people. He reminds them that although they have chosen an earthly king, they are not to forget their real ruler, the Lord. It is the Lord who has led them throughout all their history, and this they are never to forget. Then he speaks to them with words that cannot help but remind us of the covenant:

> If you will fear the Lord and serve him and hearken to his voice and not rebel against the commandment of the Lord, and if both you and the king who reigns over you will follow the Lord your God, it will be well; but if you will not hearken to the voice of the Lord, but rebel against the commandment of the Lord, then the hand of the Lord will be against you and your king. . . . Only fear the Lord, and serve him faithfully with all your heart; for consider what great things he has done for you.
>
> —1 Samuel 12:14–15, 24

SAUL REJECTED

Saul became a leader in battle for Israel against the Moabites, the Ammonites, the Edomites, and, of course, the ever-present Philistines. Men of valor were attracted to him from all Israel. Saul was king, and a king to be respected. But he was still a king under the command of God, whose will was interpreted through the prophet Samuel. As such, he was not free to do simply whatever he chose. This he soon discovered.

Samuel, as God's spokesman, gave Saul strict orders to destroy the

51

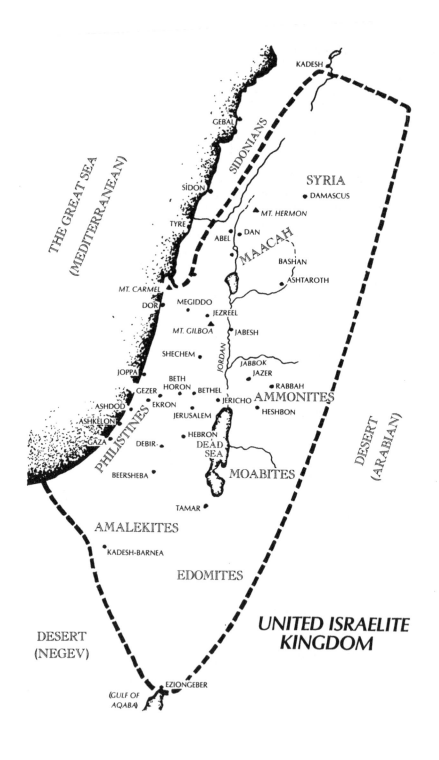

Amalekites completely in battle. Saul did not. Samuel saw this as an act of insubordination, a refusal to obey God's voice as it came through him. Samuel quickly informed Saul that God was rejecting him, that his days as king of Israel were numbered.

From that time on, Saul's whole character changed. He became more and more moody. The Spirit of the Lord was not on him as previously. It was clear that if the new kingdom were going to succeed, another leader was going to have to be found. The very life and continuance of Israel as a nation depended on it.

Whatever Saul's faults were, he was still a trailblazer of a new experiment. It was through his exploits, to a great degree, as well as through the peculiar wisdom of Samuel, that an infant kingdom was started.

Scene 5.
A GREAT NATION AND A GREAT MAN
(David)

The Lord said to Samuel, "How long will you grieve over Saul, seeing I have rejected him from being king over Israel? Fill your horn with oil, and go; I will send you to Jesse the Bethlehemite, for I have provided for myself a king among his sons."

—1 Samuel 16:1

THE ANOINTMENT OF DAVID

A lad watched his father's sheep among the gently rolling hills outside Bethlehem. He was a strong, good-looking boy. There were times when he had to be particularly watchful for the flock, lest a wolf slip in and carry off one of the sheep. And, of course, he had to be sure that the sheep had sufficient pasture and ample water. But there were other times too. Times when he could lie on the cool, green grass and let his thoughts wander near and far, wherever they wished to go. And if he wished to dream dreams of heroic exploits, as many a boy is wont to do, there was nothing to stop him.

Yet even in his wildest dreams, this lad could not possibly foresee the destiny that God had for him, a destiny that began to unfold in the quiet town of Bethlehem among the family of a man named Jesse. This was the time when Samuel, the prophet-judge, came for a visit. Ostensibly he came to conduct a service of worship in the town, and he invited all the sons of Jesse to be present. But his real reason was to anoint secretly a new king over Israel, a king who would publicly assume his office when the right time presented itself. One by one the sons of Jesse appeared before him, but none of them was chosen. Samuel began to wonder why he had come at all. "Are these all your sons?" he asked Jesse. "There is one more," replied Jesse, "but he is my youngest. He is keeping the sheep." "Get him," said Samuel.

When Samuel saw David, he felt God's Spirit stir inside of him and he knew that this was the one. He took a horn of oil and poured it over David's head, anointing him in the presence of his brothers. From this time forward, David's destiny was set. His lot and the lot of Israel were bound up together, each to the other and both to the Lord.

DAVID MEETS GOLIATH

Our story moves along and the next time we see David, he is being told by his father to take some food supplies to his brothers who are in Saul's service, fighting against the Philistines. David, who was not yet king in fact but only the king-designate, was still subject to his father's wishes. He did as he was ordered and went to the front lines with the food supplies. When he arrived, however, he did not see any fighting taking place. What he saw was despair written over all the faces of Israel's fighting men, from the humblest soldier to Saul himself. The Philistines had a mighty man of war on their side, a giant of a man. He had continually come out and challenged any Israelite soldier to single combat. So far he had had no takers. This was not surprising since the Philistine was reported to have been over nine feet tall.

Although the reaction of the Israelite soldiers was one of fear at the sight of this mammoth Philistine, David's reaction was something else. His feeling was one of contempt, almost unbelief at what was happening. He said, "Who is this uncircumcised Philistine, that he should defy the armies of the living God [1 Sam. 17:26]?"

His brothers thought he was raving, but David persisted in his contempt for the Philistine giant. His words finally came to the ears of Saul, who sent for David. Saul tried to dissuade David from what he thought was a foolhardy venture, but David would have none of it. When Saul saw that he was determined to go through with it, he gave him his own armor. This proved too heavy and awkward, however, and David took it off. Then picking up his staff, David chose five stones from a nearby brook and put them in his shepherd's bag. With his sling in his hand, he went to meet the Philistine giant.

The Philistine was aghast that one so young should be sent out to meet him, and he vented his rage (1 Samuel 17:43): "Am I a dog, that you come to me with sticks?" To this David had his own answer (1 Samuel 17:45): "You come to me with a sword and with a spear and with a javelin; but I come to you in the name of the Lord of hosts, the God of the armies of Israel, whom you have defied."

With sword drawn the Philistine advanced on David. The latter quietly put his hand into his shepherd's bag, took out a stone, and put it in his sling. Swinging the sling above his head until he had gained momentum, he slung the stone. With a whizzing sound, straight and true, it sped to its target, hitting the Philistine in the middle of the forehead. Stunned, the giant fell heavily to the ground. David raced up to him, took the Philistine's own sword and killed him, cutting off his head.

When the Philistines saw that their champion was dead, they fled in terror. And hard on their heels came the Israelites, shouting in the name of the Lord of hosts. Great and complete was the victory in Israel on that day. There was rejoicing over the whole land.

SAUL: ENEMY OF DAVID

Saul was also happy about the great victory that had been scored. But he was not happy for long. When the battle was all over and the soldiers and David and King Saul were returning, Saul heard a song that awakened the fires of jealousy in his heart. These were fires of envy that were destined to burn inside him until the day he died. As the victors were returning, women came out of Israelite villages along the route and sang (1 Samuel 18:7): "Saul has slain his thousands,/And David his ten thousands." From the moment he heard that song, Saul became an enemy of David. From that time on, David was in constant danger of losing his life. Only by God's grace and the most expert of maneuvers could David hope to remain alive.

For a time he headed the armies of Saul and stayed at the royal court where he endeavored to soothe the king's troubled spirit by playing on the lyre. During this time he formed a close friendship with Jonathan, Saul's son. However it soon became apparent that if David valued his life, he would have to put some distance between himself and Saul. Time and again the king tried to kill him. Miraculously, each time he escaped. Finally he had no choice but to leave the court and flee.

DAVID: THE FUGITIVE

David went into hiding in southern Israel and there lived the life of a fugitive. He gathered a group of men about him and, when he was not escaping from the hands of Saul, began to raid some tribes that had always been hostile to Israel. For a time he even joined the Philistines under the pretense of fighting for them against Israel. What Achish, a king of the Philistines, did not know was that every time David and his men went out to fight, they fought not against Israel but against such enemies of Israel as the Geshurites, the Girzites, and the Amalekites. Thinking that David was probably well hated by the people of Israel because of his raids, King Achish trusted him completely.

During the time that he was a fugitive, David was presented with more than one opportunity to kill Saul. This would have removed David from the cat and mouse game that Saul had been playing with his life. Yet he would not lift a finger against Saul. Why not? His own words give us the answer (1 Samuel 26:11): "The Lord forbid that I should put forth my hand against the Lord's anointed."

BITTER TEARS

Even though it would have meant peace for David, Saul's death would not come by his hand. It was, however, not long after this incident that both Saul and Jonathan did die. In the midst of a fiercely raging battle with the Israelites, the Philistines gained the upper hand and cornered the king and his son. Jonathan was killed outright by the Philistines. Just how Saul met his death is an open question. The account of 1 Samuel 31:4 tells us that Saul fell on his own sword. But the account of 2 Samuel 1:1–10 relates that a young Amalekite killed Saul at his own request after the latter was already in anguish from a fatal wound.

When the news of the death of Saul and Jonathan reached David, he wept bitter tears. Perhaps it seems strange that he should weep for one who had tried to kill him. But in David's mind, Saul was the Lord's anointed and so was very precious. No less precious to him was Jonathan, with whom he had sworn a covenant of friendship until death. Now they were both dead. Out of the depths of his sorrow, he composed a lament that deserves to be ranked with the best lyric poetry of all ages. One can feel the pathos of his heart within it. In part it reads:

> Saul and Jonathan, beloved and lovely!
> In life and in death they were not divided;
> they were swifter than eagles,
> they were stronger than lions.
>
> Ye daughters of Israel, weep over Saul,
> who clothed you daintily in scarlet,
> who put ornaments of gold upon your apparel.
>
> How are the mighty fallen
> in the midst of the battle!
>
> Jonathan lies slain upon thy high places.
> I am distressed for you, my brother Jonathan;
> very pleasant have you been to me;
> your love to me was wonderful,
> passing the love of women.
>
> How are the mighty fallen,
> and the weapons of war perished!
> —2 Samuel 1:23–27

Now was the time for the king-designate to become the king in fact. He went to the city of Hebron and was there publicly anointed king over Judah; that is, king over the southern portion of the country. Ishbosheth, Saul's son, still reigned as king over the northern portion of the country, with the help of Abner, commander of Saul's army. But Ishbosheth was a weakling; he held his position only by virtue of Abner's strength. After an argument between the two, Abner made a deal with David to support him instead of Ishbosheth. Shortly thereafter, Joab, head of David's army, killed Abner, leaving Ishbosheth completely alone. Two men who were captains in Ishbosheth's own raiding bands treacherously turned against him, killed him, and brought his head to David, thinking that this would please him. David was utterly disgusted with what they had done and had them put to death immediately.

DAVID BECOMES KING

Events then moved forward swiftly. All the elders of Israel came together at Hebron and proclaimed David king over all the land. This they did in "a covenant . . . before the Lord [2 Sam. 5:3]." How important that little insertion is. For this was not just a political event. It was a religious event. David was now king over Israel, but he had been made king not primarily because he was wise or skilled or mighty in battle. He became king over Israel by the grace of God and according to the purpose of the Almighty for the people. Great king though David became, he was ever subject to the will of God. God's prophets never let the people or their kings forget that fact. So everything they did involving the destiny of their nation, such as anointing a king, was always done "before the Lord."

No sooner had David been made king than he attacked Jerusalem, captured it, and made it the capital. Increasingly Jerusalem would be thought of not just as the central seat of government but also as the center of religion for all Israel. One of the moves to make it that was immediately executed by David. He decided to bring the ark of God to Jerusalem. In great pomp and ceremony, in song and dancing, the ark of God was brought to the city and housed in a tent.

Was David dissatisfied that the ark of God should reside in a tent? Did he wish to build a great temple in which to house it? This is the picture we get in 2 Samuel 7. But this is a very difficult chapter to understand. It is the product of at least three writers, all of whom had different viewpoints. Whatever may have been David's desire in this matter, the chapter as it now stands leaves us with three important insights:

1. The house of David would continue through future generations, blessed by God.
2. God does not really need a temple made with hands, for in the days of the wilderness wanderings God had no such abode.
3. It would be left to Solomon, son of David, to build a temple.

The reading of the chapter in its entirety reminds us again of the covenant between God and Israel. God had chosen the Israelites to do "great and terrible things," and God in turn would be their God forever.

David continued to prosper. His enemies melted before him. The boundaries of his kingdom became ever enlarged. His power steadily increased, and so did his wealth as the spoil of defeated foes poured into Israel. Israel was now a nation with which to reckon. David was in a position of power and influence such as no previous Israelite leader had ever known. It was a long way from a shepherd's tunic to the royal robes of a king. As we witness this great king, our hearts are made glad as we see him show kindness to Mephibosheth, the crippled grandson of the late King Saul. He takes him into his own household, promising to provide for him the rest of his days. We note also that "David administered justice and equity to all his people [2 Sam. 8:15]."

DAVID AND BATHSHEBA

But David was also human, and we are saddened when we read of his sin against Uriah. Uriah had a lovely wife, named Bathsheba. David fell in love with her and, in order to have her for himself, ordered Uriah put into the front line of battle, where he was killed. Nathan the prophet came to David and denounced him for what he had done. He prophesied further- more that the child to be born to him and Bathsheba would die. In agony of soul David confessed the foulness of his sin and asked forgiveness. He received forgiveness, but even as Nathan had prophesied, the child died.

Soon after this another child was born to them. This son they called Solomon.

Another heartache in the life of David involved his son Absalom. This heartache was more than personal. It involved a civil war and led very nearly to his own overthrow as king. David had many children through marriage to many wives. These wives were from tribes and cultures outside of Israel. Only in a very loose sense were these children brothers and sisters to one another. Very often they were more like strangers to one another. Because they represented different cultural and religious back- grounds, there were often jealousies and animosities among them. Thus among the household of David, there was no genuinely healthy family life, no real oneness. Nor does it appear that David did very much himself to discipline his children or strive for harmonious relations among them as a good father. Perhaps the press of kingly duties was too great. But certainly the very nature of his household, diverse as it was, made such harmony and discipline a difficult task.

DAVID AND ABSALOM

One day, Amnon, one of David's sons, forced himself on Tamar, a sister of whom Absalom was very fond. When Tamar reported the unsavory inci- dent to Absalom, he was enraged. He was further angered by his father's failure to punish Amnon. At the first opportunity, he killed Amnon to revenge Tamar's honor. Then he fled to his grandfather's house, which was out of the country, for he was afraid of what David might do to him. Finally through the intervention of Joab, David's general, there was a temporary reconciliation between father and son, but on Absalom's part it was not a sincere reconciliation. He felt that his father had wronged him by not punishing Amnon himself and by keeping him, Absalom, away from the palace for so long. Hatred burned within him and became more fierce each day.

About four years passed. At the end of that time Absalom asked permission of King David to travel to Hebron, presumably to worship God there and to fulfill a vow he had made. But this was only a ruse. Once there, he gathered around himself a small army that he had been recruiting secretly for months. Absalom found that it was not difficult to locate malcontents among the population. With false promises, he lured them to his side. When reports reached David that Absalom was about to march on Jerusalem, he and his followers quickly fled from the city and crossed over the Jordan. Absalom then took Jerusalem. Without delay, he set himself up as king.

A shrewd counselor named Ahithophel advised Absalom to pursue David immediately and kill him. This he might have succeeded in doing if it had not been for a clever espionage system that had been set up by David. For another man by the name of Hushai, a friend of David's and his foremost spy, advised Absalom to wait and attack later. Believing Hushai had betrayed David, and thinking his counsel reasonable, he followed it. Hushai's plan was carried secretly to David and his men. When Absalom and his amateurs came, David's forces were ready for them and defeated them thoroughly. The rebellion was quickly crushed.

Before the battle David had given strict orders that Absalom was not to be killed. While trying to ride his mule through the woods in the heat of battle, Absalom was caught by the neck in some low hanging tree limbs. Joab found him dangling there. Disregarding David's orders, he pierced his heart with three darts. When the battle was over, two messengers were dispatched to carry the news to David who was waiting by the gate of the city. The one messenger, Ahimaaz, outran the other and reported that the battle had been won; but about Absalom he said nothing. When the second messenger arrived, he also reported the victory. But when asked about the welfare of Absalom, he replied: "May the enemies of my lord the king, and all who rise up against you for evil, be like that young man." Stunned and overcome, King David went off by himself. As he went he sobbed aloud (2 Samuel 18:33): "O my son Absalom, my son, my son Absalom! Would I had died instead of you, O Absalom, my son, my son!"

Soon after the crushing of the rebellion, David returned to Jerusalem, and once more reigned as king over all Israel. This did not mean the end of rebellious attempts by others, nor did it mean the end of warring against outside invaders. But never again was David forced to flee from Jerusalem and never again was the kingdom in such peril while he was king. Under his rule, Israel became established as an independent kingdom, bordered on the north by the friendly kingdom of Phoenicia. Its southern territory extended to the vicinity of Beer-sheba. Its western boundary was the Great Sea (the Mediterranean) and its eastern boundary the river Jordan. In addition, the people on the other side of the Jordan had all suffered defeat at the hands of David. For the first time in history, this entire territory was under the hand of one ruler.

ISRAEL'S RISE TO PROMINENCE

Geographical growth was not the only kind of expansion however. In its peculiar position as the bridge between Europe and Africa, Israel was a commercial crossroads. As trade caravans passed through, Israel reaped the financial benefits of such commerce. David was able to accumulate a great deal of money for the nation from such trade. David is also to be credited with organizing a system of administration by which his country was governed efficiently. Under David's leadership, Israel maintained a militia to keep internal order and to discourage outside invaders. All in all, David worked something of a minor miracle in taking a weak nation at the death of Saul and building it into the powerful and efficiently ordered state that he handed over to his son Solomon.

What effect did being surrounded by great power, new wealth, and political prestige have on David's religious faith? An insight that will help us to answer this question comes to us from the incident involving David and Bathsheba. When the prophet Nathan appeared before David and accused him of wrong, what was his reaction? Did he ignore him or have his head chopped off for presuming to judge the king? Another ruler might have done one of these things. But not David. He knew that he had sinned against God and against God's higher law. King or no, he had done wrong. In deep repentance he confessed his sin. Though his was a position of power and might, he knew himself and his nation to be under the judgment of God.

A short poem that may have come directly from David gives us a glimpse into the faith that was this man's:

> The Spirit of the Lord speaks by me,
>   his word is upon my tongue.
> The God of Israel has spoken,
>   the Rock of Israel has said to me:
> When one rules justly over men
>   ruling in the fear of God,
> he dawns on them like the morning light,
>   like the sun shining forth upon a cloudless morning,

like rain that makes grass to sprout from the earth.
Yea, does not my house stand so with God?
For he has made with me an everlasting covenant,
ordered in all things and secure.

—2 Samuel 23:2–5

Near the end of the ninth century B.C., Israel had risen to a position of comparative prominence. How many Israelites at this time remembered the covenant that God had made with Israel and Israel with God? Probably only a few. But one of these must have been David, a great man who helped to fashion a great hour in the history of his nation. God, according to the Divine promise, had made Israel great. What now would Israel do with its greatness? To find that answer, we must turn to the second act in our presentation of the biblical drama.

ISRAEL IS UNFAITHFUL

Scene 1.

THE BEGINNING OF THE END

(Solomon to Rehoboam and Jeroboam)

SOLOMON: THIRD KING OF ISRAEL

David was on his deathbed. He had ruled Israel faithfully and well. But now the time of departure was at hand. The crown must rest on a younger head. A more agile mind and quicker hand must now guide the helm of Israel's destiny.

While David lay dying, some behind-the-scenes scheming was already taking place. Adonijah, one of David's many sons, was planning to make himself the new king. To this end he enlisted some powerful allies in the persons of Joab, head of the army, and Abiathar, one of the chief priests. He might have succeeded easily had not word of the plot come to the ears of Nathan, the prophet of God. Upon hearing it, he went into action urging Bathsheba, mother of Solomon, to go to David and remind him of the promise he had made that Solomon would be the next king of Israel. This she did. She told him also of Adonijah's scheme. When she had finished presenting her case, Nathan appeared and confirmed all that she had said. Now they waited in expectant silence for the word that would come from the king. At last he spoke: "As the Lord lives, who has redeemed my soul out of every adversity, as I swore to you by the Lord, the God of Israel, saying, 'Solomon your son shall reign after me, and he shall sit upon my throne in my stead'; even so will I do this day [1 Kings 1:29-30]."

David had spoken. With great fanfare Solomon, riding on the king's own donkey, was taken to Gihon by Nathan the prophet, Zadok the priest, and Benaiah, accompanied by the Cherethites and the Pelethites, the crack unit of fighting men most intensely loyal to David. There before the assembled people, Zadok the priest took the horn of oil out of the tent and anointed Solomon. The trumpets blew and the people shouted, "Long live King Solomon!" Thus Solomon began a reign that was to be filled with splendor such as Israel had never seen before and has not seen since.

With the proclamation of Solomon as king, the cause of Adonijah completely collapsed. However Solomon agreed to spare his life on condition that he behave himself. His failure to keep this condition led to his eventual death (1 Kings 2:13-25).

David's Charge to Solomon

Just before David died, he charged his son Solomon to live uprightly, to follow God's commandments, and to perform certain deeds in his behalf. This charge is found in 1 Kings 2. The second part of the charge directs Solomon to avenge the bloodguiltiness that had come on the house of David when Joab without good reason slew both Abner and Amasa. Solomon was also directed to avenge the curse that rested on the royal house from the lips of Shimei and finally to remember the oath of goodwill that David had made the sons of Barzillai. In remembrance of this sacred charge from his father and according to the prevailing custom of that time, Soloman saw to it that both Joab and Shimei were put to death.

The first part of this charge portrays David as urging his son to keep faithfully the commandments and ordinances of the Lord. Solomon is told that only thus will his reign prosper and the nation be blessed. And so we read:

> I am about to go the way of all the earth. Be strong, and show yourself a man, and keep the charge of the Lord your God, walking in his ways and keeping his statutes, the commandments, his ordinances, and his testimonies, as it is written in the law of Moses, that you may prosper in all that you do and wherever you turn; that the Lord may establish his word which he spoke concerning me, saying, "If your sons take heed to their way, to walk before me in faithfulness with all their heart and with all their soul, there shall not fail you a man on the throne of Israel."
>
> —1 Kings 2:2-4

The Deuteronomic Editor

These verses are the work of the Deuteronomic editor who compiled the history of Israel as we find it in 1 and 2 Kings. Being a devoutly religious man and zealous for the law of God, this editor was always at pains to point out that as Israel kept the commandments of God, it was strong and virile; as it did not keep them, it was weak and vulnerable. By this we see that the *covenant* faith was very much a part of the man who edited this history of Israel. We do not know his name, but we do know that the point of view of this editor is that which is found in the book of Deuteronomy.

This book, meaning literally "second law," became the basis for a moral and spiritual cleanup campaign in Judah around 600 B.C. It was at this time that 1 and 2 Kings were written. This history of Israel and Judah was written under the influence of the great moral and spiritual ideas found in the book of Deuteronomy. If one were to sum up these ideas in capsule form, they would look something like this:

1. The Lord God of Israel was alone to be worshiped and served. All foreign gods and idols were an abomination.
2. The only real place for God to be worshiped was in Jerusalem; not in shrines scattered throughout the country.
3. Justice and mercy were to be shown to the poor.

As the Deuteronomic editor (called D for short) penned this history of Israel and Judah, he judged every ruler from Solomon to his time of writing by how faithfully each one measured up to the above principles. In other words, the D editor was applying the measuring rod of the covenant to the history of his people. As they kept that covenant, they were strong. As they neglected it, they were weak. So we see that it is no new idea to look at the biblical drama from the perspective of Israel's covenant responsibility to God. This is the very thing that the D editor himself was doing. And as we shall see somewhat later, it is also the way in which the prophets of Israel looked at the life of their people.

Bearing in mind then the particular viewpoint of the D editor, let us take up the history of Israel as we find it unfolding in the reign of Solomon.

Solomon got off to a good start. Sensing the heavy responsibility that rested upon him, he decided that his main desire was for wisdom to handle the affairs of the nation. In his prayer to God, he made this clear:

> And thy servant is in the midst of thy people whom thou hast chosen, a great people, that cannot be numbered or counted for multitude. Give thy servant therefore an understanding mind to govern thy people, that I may discern between good and evil; for who is able to govern this thy great people?
>
> —1 Kings 3:8-9

The Building of the Temple

That Solomon did possess unusual wisdom and understanding is attested by wise administration of the kingdom, by the intricate plans set forth for the building of the temple, and by his dealings with persons. Particularly in the eyes of the D editor, the building of the temple was of utmost importance. Why? Because this tended to centralize the worship of God in one place—in Jerusalem, the Holy City. This event decreased the importance of other local shrines throughout the country. From this time forward when Israelites worshiped God, even if they could not always travel to Jerusalem, they could face toward the holy city and "pray toward this place [1 Kings 8:30]." All of which would help to keep corrupt elements from entering into the worship of the one God. The great temple of Jerusalem would discredit the idols in local high places in other sections of the country, and the worship of God would be kept pure.

There can be little doubt as far as the D editor was concerned that the building of the temple was Solomon's great contribution to the history and religion of Israel. The temple was a gleaming white stone structure over 100 feet long, 30 feet wide, and 45 feet high. Set on the top of a hill and silhouetted against the sky, it must have been a truly awesome sight. Yet it was not the external grandeur of the temple that was of prime importance. Its chief importance was that it represented the faithfulness of the people of Israel to their God and the covenant that God had made with them and that they had made with God. The bringing of the ark of the covenant to reside in the innermost part of the temple was meant to remind all Israel of this fact. Unless the temple really represented an "integrity of heart and uprightness" among the people, it would be but a cold and barren edifice doomed to destruction. And if it were doomed to destruction, then doomed with it would be the nation also. This concern of the D editor is pointedly reflected in the reply ascribed to the Lord in answer to Solomon's prayer of dedication. Thus we read:

> And the Lord said to him, "I have heard your prayer and your supplication, which you have made before me; I have consecrated this house which you have built, and put my name there for ever; my eyes and my heart will be there for all time. And as for you, if you will walk before me, as David your father walked, with integrity of heart and uprightness, doing according to all that I have commanded you, and keeping my statutes and my ordinances, then I will establish your royal throne over Israel for ever, as I promised David your father, saying, 'There shall not fail you a man upon the throne of Israel.' But if you turn aside from following me, you or your children, and do not keep my commandments and my statutes which I have set before you, but go and serve other gods and worship them, then I will cut off Israel from the land which I have given them; and the house which I have consecrated for my name I will cast out of my sight; and Israel will become a proverb and a byword among all peoples. And this house will become a heap of ruins; everyone passing by it will be astonished, and will hiss; and they will say, 'Why has the Lord done thus to this land and to this house?' Then they will say, 'Because they forsook the Lord their God who brought their fathers out of the land of Egypt, and laid hold on other gods, and worshiped them and served them; therefore the Lord has brought all this evil upon them.'"

—1 Kings 9:3–9

SOLOMON: IDOLATRY AND CORRUPTION

It would be well if the story of Solomon ended right at this point with his being remembered for the one great accomplishment of the building of the temple. But this is not the end of his story. Solomon himself stands condemned as one who went after other gods. He took to himself wives from all the nations round about. At the same time, he took also the customs and practices of the lands from which his wives came. This included, among other things, their religious practices. He built an altar in honor of Chemosh, the god of the Moabites, and another in honor of Molech, the god of the Ammonites.

In the end he not only infested the land with these religious impurities, but he himself worshiped these idols of stone. God became just another god among many in Solomon's collection. Added to his spiritual corruption was a moral stagnancy, the troublesome activities of Hadad and Rezon (1 Kings 11:14–25), and the chafing at the bit of the people of the north over Solomon's policy of "forced labor." All these things together made for a situation that was ripe for revolt.

> And the Lord was angry with Solomon, because his heart had turned away from the Lord, the God of Israel. . . . Therefore the Lord said to Solomon, "Since this has been your mind and you have not kept my covenant and my statutes which I have commanded you, I will surely tear the kingdom from you and will give it to your servant. Yet for the sake of David your father I will not do it in your days, but I will tear it out of the hand of your son. However I will not tear away all the kingdom; but I will give one tribe to your son, for the sake of David my servant and for the sake of Jerusalem which I have chosen."
> —1 Kings 11:9, 11–13

It is rather tragic that the one whose name we laud in connection with the great temple must also be remembered by us as one who turned away from God. Yet it is so, and no amount of wishing otherwise will change it. This is no Hollywood success story. The events as we meet them in the Bible do not always have a happy ending. Just so here. In ignominy Solomon quietly slips out of our story, to be mentioned only one more time in a brief obituary (1 Kings 11:42–43): "And the time that Solomon reigned in Jerusalem over all Israel was forty years. And Solomon slept with his fathers, and was buried in the city of David his father; and Rehoboam his son reigned in his stead."

REHOBOAM AND JEROBOAM: A CRUCIAL DEMAND

Rehoboam, son of Solomon. What would his ascending to the throne of Israel mean? Would he continue the policies of his father? Or would he adopt quite different policies? An answer was not long in coming. When he went to the town of Shechem to be made king, a delegation of Israelites paid him an official visit. The spokesman for the delegation was one called Jeroboam.

Jeroboam had at one time been in charge of the "forced labor" that Solomon recruited from Israel. But he was not happy in this job. He did not like to see his countrymen impressed against their will into such hard service on the pet projects of the king. This was, in effect, another kind of slavery. He wanted none of it. One day he was met out in the open country by a prophet of the Lord, named Ahijah. The prophet did a strange thing. He took his cloak, which was brand new, and tore it into twelve pieces. He took ten of the pieces and gave them to Jeroboam, telling him that these ten pieces represented ten of the twelve tribes of Israel. These ten tribes would be given into his hands, and he would be king over them. Only Judah (included Judah and Simeon) would remain in the hands of the house of Solomon. Whereupon Ahijah went on his way, and Jeroboam returned to his tasks. When Solomon learned of this brewing revolt, he tried to nip it in the bud. But too late. Jeroboam had already fled into Egypt.

Now Solomon was dead and Jeroboam was back speaking for the delegation that confronted Rehoboam. His request was simple (1 Kings 12:4): "Your father made our yoke heavy. Now therefore lighten the hard service of your father and his heavy yoke upon us, and we will serve you."

Rehoboam listened to their request and asked them to come back in three days, at which time he would give them an answer. He then consulted with his counselors on the matter. The older men, who had known how hard Solomon was with the people, advised him to go easy, to let up and to heed the request of the people. The younger men who had grown up with him, not having the wisdom of years or the appreciation of the plight of the people, advised him to deal even more harshly with the people. On the third day, Rehoboam gave his answer (1 Kings 12:14): "My father made your yoke heavy, but I will add to your yoke; my father chastised you with whips, but I will chastise you with scorpions."

THE KINGDOM DIVIDES

The people had asked and had received an answer. Now there was only one alternative. The ten tribes of the north, now to be called Israel, revolted and separated themselves from the rule of Rehoboam. Henceforth he reigned over only the Southern Kingdom of Judah. As prophesied by Ahijah, Jeroboam was proclaimed king over Israel. This was indeed a tragic day in the history of the Hebrew nation. Faithful to the covenant promise, God had made of this people a great nation. Their own unfaithfulness to the covenant was turning this promise into a judgment upon them. The splendor and glory that had been Israel's would be no more.

A Calf of Gold

Jeroboam immediately set to the task of putting things in order in the Northern Kingdom of Israel. So that the people of his realm would not feel compelled to go down to Jerusalem to worship, he built his own shrines at Bethel in southern Israel and at Dan in northern Israel. He made a calf of gold to be placed in each shrine and then said: "Behold your gods, O Israel, who brought you up out of the land of Egypt [1 Kings 12:28]." In addition he appointed priests from among the people.

It does not take a great deal of imagination to figure out what the D editor of this story thought about Jeroboam's actions. They would of course horrify anyone whose cardinal principle was the worship of God alone. The judgment of the D editor can easily be seen in the following:

> Jeroboam did not turn from his evil way, but made priests for the high places again from among all the people; any who would, he consecrated to be priests of the high places. And this thing became sin to the house of Jeroboam, so as to cut it off and to destroy it from the face of the earth.
>
> —1 Kings 13:33–34

The prophet Ahijah had looked to Jeroboam as the first king of the ten tribes of Israel. But his hope did not last long. It did not take long for Jeroboam to make for himself "other gods." In words that come mostly from the D editor, Ahijah forecasts the destruction of the whole house of Jeroboam, a destruction that begins with the death of Jeroboam's beloved son, Abijah (1 Kings 14:1–20). Jeroboam reigned for twenty-two years in Israel; yet during all those years the word that Ahijah spoke to his wife concerning his son must have rung in his ears, tormenting him day and night (1 Kings 14:12): "Arise therefore, go to your house. When your feet enter the city, the child shall die."

The death of his son not only brought back a sad memory. It may very well have served as a symbol to him of what lay in store for Israel. After twenty-two years of kingship, Jeroboam "slept with his fathers, and Nadab his son reigned in his stead."

Idolatry and Plunder

In the Southern Kingdom of Judah, Rehoboam reigned for seventeen years. Yet even though the great temple was in Jerusalem as a constant reminder of the Lord God of hosts, the religious situation in Judah did not fare any better than it did in the north. Local shrines were built, as the Bible says, "on every high hill," and corrupt worship practices were engaged in throughout the country. The people "did according to all the abominations of the nations which the Lord drove out before the people of Israel." During Rehoboam's reign, Shishak, king of Egypt, came up to

Jerusalem and plundered the temple, carrying off its treasures and shields of gold. Judah was powerless to stop him. To say the least, Rehoboam's seventeen years as ruler add up to a bleak and dismal picture. After his death, Abijam his son reigned in his stead.

In Solomon we saw the pinnacle of Israel's glory and power and prestige. We saw also in his reign the swift descent from that pinnacle. In Rehoboam we witnessed the final break, never to be healed, between north and south. In Jeroboam we beheld only too quickly a departure from the commandments of the Lord. All told, this time in Israel's history must be regarded as a tragic time. It was a time when God's covenant was forgotten; a time when a nation was catapulting itself toward its own destruction. It was the beginning of the end.

Scene 2.
MIGHTIER THAN KINGS
(Elijah, Micaiah, and Elisha)

From the split of the United Kingdom in 922 B.C. to the fall of the Northern Kingdom in 722 B.C., Israel had no fewer than nineteen kings. Judah, the Southern Kingdom, was not conquered until about the year 587 B.C. During that time it had a total of twenty rulers. Of these only a few stand out as having influenced significantly the history of Israel and Judah.

The D editor who put this history together felt there were only a few who did the country much good. To all the kings of Israel, and to over half the kings of Judah, he applied one formula time and again: "He did what was evil in the sight of the Lord, walking in the way of his father and in his sin which he made Israel to sin."

Again, we must remember the standard by which the D editor judged these kings. If they allowed religious shrines to be set up around the country and encouraged the worship of idols and false gods, then of course this was regarded by him as a very great evil. For it was his conviction that only the Lord God was worthy to be worshiped. It was God who had led the people out of bondage in Egypt. It was God who had made a covenant with them, choosing them as a special people. It was God who had led them into this land and had driven out their adversaries before them. It was not the gods of the Canaanites or the Moabites or the Ammonites or any other god. It was the Lord of hosts, the God of Abraham, Isaac, and Jacob. Any king who chose to forget this and encouraged devotion to other gods could only be considered by the D editor as doing "what was evil in the sight of the Lord."

SOME GOOD RULES

The situation, however, was not all bad. There were rulers, especially in Judah, who were concerned for the worship of God, and God only. And to that end, they instituted a reform, some with more enthusiasm and some with less. King Asa reigned for forty years in Judah, from 913 to 873 B.C. He put a stop to idol worship and to immoral practices associated with such worship. So dedicated was he to the worship of God that he even deposed his own mother from the queenship because she worshiped the god Asherah. Jehoshaphat, Asa's son, was also zealous for the purity of Judah's worship; he carried on where his father left off. Jehoash (837–800), Amaziah (800–783), Azariah, known also as Uzziah (783–742), Jotham (742–735), Hezekiah (715–687) and Josiah (640–609) were all kings of Judah, each of whom by virtue of his devotion to the pure worship of God earned this tribute from the editor: "And he did what was right in the eyes of the Lord [2 Kings 18:3; 22:2]."

A special tribute, however, was reserved for both Hezekiah and Josiah. Their reforms, especially those of Josiah, were more drastic than any others. For they not only did away with idols and cultic practices but they destroyed the various shrines that existed outside Jerusalem. And, of course, this certainly met with the approval of the D editor, who believed that God should be worshiped only at the temple in Jerusalem.

By the same token, it did not matter how great any ruler of the Northern Kingdom was. He received no accolade from the editor, because he encouraged worship away from Jerusalem.

Jehu (842–815), who wiped out all the worshipers of the god Baal in the land of Israel, came closest to receiving a verbal pat on the back from the Deuteronomist. Yet, not quite. He was still condemned as one who "was not careful to walk in the law of the Lord the God of Israel with all his heart; he did not turn from the sins of Jeroboam, which he made Israel to sin [2 Kings 10:31]."

This was a turbulent time in the history of Israel and Judah. It was a time when the people's allegiance to the God of Sinai was almost forgotten. And yet not completely forgotten. For God would not let the Israelites forget. To ensure that they would not, God raised up prophets, who would speak to the people for God. These were persons who would remind their hearers that the people of Israel and Judah were a covenant people. It is these persons, mightier than kings, whose words and deeds shout to us from the pages of the Bible. It is they who carry the torch of Israel's religious genius through these chaotic years and keep it burning when all around them there is spiritual and moral darkness. It is to these prophets that we now turn. It is through their eyes that we need to examine the relationship between God and God's people.

ELIJAH

Elijah, one of the early prophets for God, steps on the stage of history at the time when Ahab is king of Israel. Ahab knows Elijah and thoroughly despises him. Although the king liked to think of himself as loyal to God, he gave mostly lip service to Yahweh. His real sympathies were with one of the Baals, gods of fertility, for whom he even built a special altar. In all this there is no doubt that he was influenced by his wife Jezebel, daughter of Ethbaal, king of the Sidonians. For she herself was an ardent worshiper of the Baals.

Ahab, therefore, held little love for Elijah, who by his very presence accused the king of disloyalty to Yahweh. For three years there had been a severe famine over the whole land. Ahab put the blame squarely on Elijah. In fact, he sent spies to look for him even outside the borders of the country. Somehow Ahab felt that if he could only find Elijah, this cursed famine would come to an end.

Almost three years passed. On a certain day Ahab and the overseer of his household, Obadiah, were foraging through the countryside in order to find grass for the horses and mules. Ahab went in one direction, Obadiah in another. As the latter searched diligently by spring and valley, he suddenly stopped in his tracks. At that moment he looked as though he had seen a ghost. For right in front of him was Elijah, the man for whom Ahab had been searching. Obadiah fell on his face and asked, scarcely believing his eyes, "Is it you, my lord Elijah?" The prophet was quick to assure him that it was so. Then Elijah told Obadiah to find Ahab and to bring the king to him. But, at that simple request, Obadiah protested. In effect, he said to Elijah, "What are you trying to do, get me killed? You know as well as I do that if I tell him I have found you, after all this time, and then he comes and you are not here, he will kill me!"

"Don't worry," replied Elijah. "This time I will not disappear. I will be right here when he comes." With that assurance, Obadiah left to find the king.

When Ahab finally appeared, his first words to Elijah indicated what he thought of the prophet: "Is it you, you troubler of Israel?" But Elijah retorted (1 Kings 18:18): "I have not troubled Israel; but you have, and your father's house, because you have forsaken the commandments of the Lord and followed the Baals."

A CONTEST ON MOUNT CARMEL

With that, Elijah proposed a contest. To Mount Carmel, a high promontory jutting out into the Mediterranean Sea, were to come four hundred and fifty prophets of Baal, four hundred prophets of Asherah, Elijah, the people of Israel,and the king. The king accepted the proposal. On the chosen day, they came together from near and far and Elijah addressed them, saying (1 Kings 18:21): "How long will you go limping with two different opinions? If the Lord is God, follow him; but if Baal, then follow him."

He then set forth the rules of the contest. The four hundred and fifty prophets of Baal were to take a bull, cut it in pieces, set it on their own altar over the wood, but put no fire to it. Elijah was to do the same. Each would then call on the name of his god. The god that answered by fire was to be acknowledged as the true god. After the rules were laid down, he invited the prophets of Baal to proceed with their sacrifice first. So they took one of the bulls, prepared it as prescribed, laid it on the altar, and began to call on the name of their god. "O Baal, answer us!" they cried. This they did from morning to noon. The scripture reports the results in these terse words: "But there was no voice, and no one answered [1 Kings 18:26]."

Yet, they did not give up but limped about the altar making all kinds of weird incantations. Elijah sat to one side meanwhile, watching all that happened. Finally, he could resist no longer. He shouted out to the prophets of Baal these mocking words (1 Kings 18:27): "Cry aloud, for he is a god; either he is musing, or he has gone aside, or he is on a journey, or perhaps he is asleep and must be awakened."

With that their shouting grew fiercer. In a frenzy of excitement, they began to dance and jump around, cutting themselves until the blood gushed from them. In this way, they hoped to arouse their god. Again, the scripture itself puts it best of all. In 1 Kings 18:29, we read: "And as midday passed, they raved on until the time of the offering of the oblation, but there was no voice; no one answered, no one heeded."

"THE LORD IS GOD"

Then it was Elijah's turn. He prepared his sacrifice in the same way as those who had preceded him, with one exception. He ordered four jars filled with water and had the contents poured over the altar three times until the water filled the trench that encircled it. Then Elijah approached the altar. Everything was still. It was the kind of quiet that comes spontaneously over a multitude when those present sense that something great, something wonderful, is about to happen. The prophet raised his head and lifted his outstretched arms toward heaven. In a voice both firm and serene, he said:

O Lord, God of Abraham, Isaac, and Israel, let it be known this day that thou art God in Israel, and that I am thy servant, and that I have done all these things at thy word. Answer me, O Lord, answer me,

that this people may know that thou, O Lord, art God, and that thou
hast turned their hearts back.

—1 Kings 18:36–37

A flash of lightning cut the sky in two. The sacrifice—the wood, the
stones, the dust and the water in the trench—were all consumed by the
"fire of the Lord." For a brief moment there was again silence, the silence
of reverent wonder before so great a majesty. This was followed by a great
shout. The people fell on their faces and cried with one voice: "The Lord,
he is God; the Lord, he is God [1 Kings 18:39]."

So in dramatic fashion the people were called to remembrance. This
was the remembrance of the God of Israel, who had led their ancestors
out of bondage in Egypt, who had covenanted with them to be their God,
and who had chosen them to be a special people. For this cause, the cause
of remembrance, God had put an Elijah in their midst.

This was not the only incident in the life of Elijah, but it was a crucial
one. Elijah had his times of weakness, lack of courage, and confusion.
Some of these are recorded in 1 Kings 19:1–18. At such times he withdrew
to a place of seclusion. But from his moments of retreat he emerged as a
strong spokesman for God in the midst of the affairs of the nation.

Thus his life was lived. Nor was the influence of that life over at his
death. Sometime before he had appointed one to be his disciple. The sign
of that appointment was the casting of his own mantle upon the other. The
symbol of his authority was thus passed on. When, in the picturesque
imagery of the biblical story, Elijah "went up by a whirlwind into heaven,"
the mantle became Elisha's. Upon Elisha, even as he had requested, a
"double portion" of the spirit of Elijah rested. Before taking up the story
of Elisha, however, there is a prophet of God who must command our
attention, even if only for a brief while. He is mentioned in 1 Kings 22. Yet
that one chapter is enough to reveal him as a man of courage. His name is
Micaiah.

MICAIAH

Ahab had his greedy eyes on the city of Ramoth-gilead. It so happened
that this city belonged to Syria. One day when Jehoshaphat, the king of
Judah, paid him a visit, Ahab suggested that they make war against it. He
wanted to know if Jehoshaphat would be willing to join in the campaign
with him. Since Israel was so much larger than Judah, Jehoshaphat could
only reply meekly: "I am as you are, my people as your people, my horses
as your horses [1 Kings 22:4]."

But then Jehoshaphat had another idea. He did not want to rush into
such an action pell-mell, so he suggested that Ahab inquire first for a word
from the Lord in the matter. So Ahab summoned the four hundred court

74

prophets. They told him: "Go up; for the Lord will give it into the hand of the king."

This did not entirely satisfy Jehoshaphat. Again he made a request of Ahab, this time right in front of the court prophets: "Is there not here another prophet of the Lord of whom we may inquire?" Ahab squirmed a bit, and answered: "There is yet one man by whom we may inquire of the Lord, Micaiah the son of Imlah." Then he added quickly: "But I hate him, for he never prophesies good concerning me, but evil [1 Kings 22:8]."

Micaiah was finally summoned. The two kings were sitting in royal regalia before the gate of the city. In front of them were the four hundred prophets of the court, urging Ahab to go up to battle against Ramoth-gilead. Surrounding them were the members of the court. Beyond them were the people of the city. In the middle of this scene stood Micaiah. Without hesitation, Ahab put the question to him: "Micaiah, shall we go to Ramoth-gilead to battle, or shall we forbear?" Micaiah toyed with him a little: "Go up and triumph; the Lord will give it into the hand of the king."

Ahab was enraged. He knew that Micaiah was deliberately making fun of him. "How many times shall I adjure you that you speak to me nothing but the truth in the name of the Lord?"

Whereupon, Micaiah gave the real word of God he had intended all along (1 Kings 22:17): "I saw all Israel scattered upon the mountains, as sheep that have no shepherd; and the Lord said, 'These have no master; let each return to his home in peace.'"

So Micaiah gave the very unpopular advice that they should not go into battle against Ramoth-gilead, that this was against God's will. He further accused the court prophets of having a lying spirit within them. For this remark he was struck on the cheek by Zedekiah, chief of the court prophets. Whereupon Ahab ordered Micaiah thrown into jail, saying, "Put this fellow in prison, and feed him with scant fare of bread and water, until I come in peace."

Before he could be dragged away, Micaiah shouted: "If you return in peace, the Lord has not spoken by me [1 Kings 22:28]."

As it turned out, God had spoken through this man of courage. The Syrians routed the armies of Israel and Judah, and Ahab died of a wound received in the battle.

It was seldom a popular thing to speak God's word, especially when the spiritual darkness was so great. Yet Micaiah stands as one of those dedicated servants who fearlessly spoke the word of the Lord to his people.

ELISHA

No prophet was more involved in the life of Israel than Elisha. He lived during the reign of at least six of the kings of Israel. His activity extended from Ahab, when he was appointed by Elijah as his disciple, to Joash, during whose reign he died. The tales told concerning him are many and varied. All sorts of "wonder stories" have revolved about him.

Of the many events of Israel's history in which Elisha was involved, one is of particular interest to all who are concerned with the tracing of the history of the covenant. This event is a judgment on Israel, and especially on the descendants of Ahab because they had disregarded their covenant with the living God. Elisha is involved in the event only as its instigator. He called one of the sons of the prophets to him, gave him a flask of oil, and told him to go to Ramoth-gilead where he was directed to search for Jehu, the son of Jehoshaphat. Jehu had charge of the armies of Israel at this outpost while the king was recovering in Jezreel from wounds suffered in battle. When he had found Jehu, the prophet chosen by Elisha was to pour the oil over Jehu's head according to the custom of anointing and say: "Thus says the Lord, I anoint you king over Israel [2 Kings 9:3]."

The prophet did as Elisha directed him. He went to Ramoth-gilead, found Jehu, and anointed him king, speaking the words he had been told to speak. However, more words are included in the account of the anointing than came from Elisha's original directions. The amplified version probably came from the D editor of 1 and 2 Kings. As always, this editor judged all rulers by their faithfulness to the God of Israel. In the eyes of the editor, Ahab was one of the worst offenders of all. Thus, whatever befell Ahab and his house could only be interpreted as God's judgment upon them. Anticipating this judgment, he inserted in 2 Kings 9:7-10 these words which are meant to act both as a guide for Jehu's actions and a prophecy of doom for the house of Ahab:

> And you shall strike down the house of Ahab your master, that I may avenge on Jezebel the blood of my servants the prophets, and the blood of all the servants of the Lord. For the whole house of Ahab shall perish; and I will cut off from Ahab every male, bond or free, in Israel. And I will make the house of Ahab like the house of Jeroboam the son of Nebat, and like the house of Baasha the son of Ahijah. And the dogs shall eat Jezebel in the territory of Jezreel, and none shall bury her.
>
> —2 Kings 9:7-10

After his anointment as king, Jehu lost no time getting into action. He rode like a madman in his chariot to Jezreel. On the way there, he killed both Joram, the king of Israel who was a son of Ahab, and Ahaziah, king of Judah. Then he hurried on to Jezreel, where Jezebel, the scheming, cunning, pagan wife of Ahab, waited for him. She had fostered the worship of Baal throughout all Israel; she had slaughtered the prophets of Yahweh whenever she could get her hands on them; and she had caused a perfectly innocent man by the name of Naboth to be killed, so that Ahab could confiscate his vineyard. Now her time had come. And she knew it.

When Jehu drove into the gate of the city, Jezebel saw him from the palace window. She shouted to him: "Is it peace, you Zimri, murderer of your master?" With that, Jehu shouted orders to some men who were in the palace, and they threw Jezebel down into the courtyard. Then Jehu went inside to eat. When he later sent servants outside to take her up and bury her, they found almost nothing. The dogs, according to prophecy, had arrived there first.

Not one to do half a job, Jehu had the seventy sons of Ahab rounded up and killed also. Finally in an effort to bring some restoration of the worship of Yahweh, he gathered together as many worshipers of Baal as he could find. He did so under the ruse of holding a great feast in Baal's honor. But when the temple was filled, Jehu sent in eighty of his warriors who killed everyone who worshiped the Baal. Then he tore down the temple of Baal and turned it into a toilet.

Although the D editor cannot bring himself to appreciate Jehu unqualifiedly, he does praise him for his religious reforms and for his destruction of the house of Ahab. In this, the D editor represents him as doing the will of Yahweh.

Elijah, Micaiah, and Elisha glow as beacon lights in a time that was religiously dark and politically turbulent. The Lord God of Israel was either totally ignored or set alongside other gods. The covenant which God had made with this people was all but forgotten. The moral life of the people was at a low ebb. Political trickery, self-interest, and the pursuit of pleasure seemed to dominate the thinking of the time. Nevertheless, in the middle of all this we find persons of courage and conviction and faith. If nowhere else in this period, we find that at least in them the light of the covenant continued to shine. Though the darkness was intense in Israel, even greater lights were about to shine forth. And their light has not been extinguished to this day.

Scene 3.
GOD'S GIANTS
(Amos, Hosea, Isaiah, Micah, and Jeremiah to the Fall of the Northern and Southern Kingdoms)

AMOS THE RANCHER

Tekoa was a little town in Judea, some six miles south of the great city of Jerusalem. It had no particular claim to fame. It was a border outpost for the defense of the Holy City. Situated in the middle of very hilly country, it was not at all suited to the raising of crops. But around it was good grazing land. Sheepherding was one of the main occupations of that area.

Indeed, it was a sheepherder that gave this quiet town its greatest renown.

In all likelihood, Amos was a moderately well-to-do sheep rancher. He was not rich, not by any means. It would be difficult to see how anyone living in such a semi-barren region as that surrounding Tekoa could be truly wealthy. The fact that Amos took care also of a grove of sycamore trees to add to his income would seem to tell us that he was not overly prosperous. Nevertheless, it is safe to say that he was comfortable. This is important to understand, when later we note some of the things that Amos said to the people. As one who was not himself poor, he spoke in behalf of those who had been "ground into the dust."

AMOS VISITS SAMARIA

It was business that took him to the bustling city of Samaria, capital of the Northern Kingdom of Israel. Israel was at that time much more powerful than Judah. Samaria was considered the political and commercial crossroads of the land. So it was natural for Amos to avoid Jerusalem and to journey from Tekoa to Samaria. The middle of the eighth century B.C. saw Israel in its heyday. Jeroboam II was on the throne. Politically speaking, he was a very able monarch. The boundaries of the kingdom were extended, cities once held by Syria were retaken, and even Damascus, the capital of Syria, paid tribute to Israel. Having command of the important trade routes meant an influx of commerce and wealth. The great power of Assyria had withdrawn from the scene because of troubles elsewhere, leaving the kingdom of Israel riding high and mighty.

To say the least, this was a time of confidence and satisfaction in Israel. It was also a time when people could easily blind themselves to the festering conditions of their society. This is exactly what most did, but not the ruddy-faced rancher from the southern hills.

When Amos came to Samaria, and had a chance to look around him, he saw conditions that made him blush with shame. Was this really happening in Israel? Was this happening to the chosen people of God?

UNJUST PRACTICES IMMORAL

Men and women and children were sold as slaves in the marketplace, because they could not pay a debt that amounted to no more than the price of a pair of shoes. Creditors were so greedy for gain that they wore the garments of those in their debt, garments which were only supposed to be given into their care until the debtor could pay. Religious prostitution was practiced in the temple of God, a cult practice adopted from one of the pagan religions of the land. Thus was the name of God profaned throughout the land.

Fat, indolent women had nothing to do but lie upon their couches all day, with no care for the needy or oppressed, concerned only that their

physical wants be gratified. This was Amos' stinging condemnation of
them:

> "Hear this word, you cows of Bashan,
>> who are in the mountain of Samaria,
> who oppress the poor, who crush the needy,
>> who say to their husbands,
>>> 'Bring, that we may drink!'
> The Lord God has sworn by his holiness
>> that, behold, the days are coming upon you,
> when they shall take you away with hooks,
>> even the last of you with fishhooks.
> And you shall go out through the breaches,
>> every one straight before her;
>> and you shall be cast forth into Harmon," says the Lord.
>> —Amos 4:1–3

The rich became richer, and the poor became poorer. The rich, according to Amos, were turning "aside the needy in the gate." So obsessed by making money were the merchants of the town that they could hardly wait for the sabbath and the holy days to end. Then they could get back to dealing in false weights and balances, cheating the simple and selling them the leftovers of the wheat.

UNHOLY WORSHIP

Added to all this was the sham worship of God at the holy places. Great feasts, the showing off of wealth and position, the gratifying of lust, the savory sacrifices—all these were enjoyed under the pretense of worshiping God. In truth, it was not God they were worshiping; it was themselves. As far as they were concerned, worship at the holy places was just another occasion for doing what they wanted. In short, a trip to the religious shrines at Bethel or Gilgal was just another excuse for self-indulgence. Knowing this full well, Amos ridiculed the shameful practices of the people with scathing sarcasm:

> "Come to Bethel, and transgress;
>> to Gilgal, and multiply transgression;
> bring your sacrifices every morning,
>> your tithes every three days;
> offer a sacrifice of thanksgiving of that which is leavened,
>> and proclaim freewill offerings, publish them;
>> for so you love to do, O people of Israel!" says the Lord God.
>> —Amos 4:4–5

Confronted by a diseased society, Amos felt himself divinely appointed to thunder the judgment of the Almighty upon it. Israel had broken the law

79

of God in every abominable way imaginable. Its people had committed all kinds of immoralities. Justice was dependent upon how much money one had; the equality of desert days had turned into a caste system favoring the well-to-do; the pure religion of Yahweh had been corrupted by the religious practices of Israel's neighbors; and the worship of God had become a shallow, meaningless ceremony. Yahweh had chosen Israel to be the carrier of the covenant; through them were all nations to be blessed. But Israel had trampled that covenant in the dust. What, now, would be the consequences of such infidelity?

> You only have I known
> of all the families of the earth;
> therefore I will punish you
> for all your iniquities.
> —Amos 3:2

JUDGMENT

Punishment! Destruction! Judgment! This was the word of the Lord to Israel as it came through Amos. These are the words that issued forth from his mouth:

> For thus says the Lord God:
> "The city that went forth a thousand
> shall have a hundred left,
> and that which went forth a hundred
> shall have ten left
> to the house of Israel."
>
> He who made the Pleiades and Orion,
> and turns deep darkness into the morning,
> and darkens the day into night, . . .
> the Lord is his name,
> who makes destruction flash forth against the strong,
> so that destruction comes upon the fortress.
>
> You have built houses of hewn stone,
> but you shall not dwell in them;
> you have planted pleasant vineyards,
> but you shall not drink their wine.
>
> For behold, the Lord commands,
> and the great house shall be smitten into fragments,
> and the little house into bits.
>
> "For behold, I will raise up against
> you a nation,
> O house of Israel," says the Lord, the God of hosts;

80

> "and they shall oppress you from the entrance of Hamath
> to the Brook of the Arabah."
> —Amos 5:3, 8–9, 11; 6:11, 14

In chapters 7, 8, and 9 of the book of Amos are recorded five visions that are attributed to the prophet. Each of these visions has something to do with the fate of Israel. They may have been suggested by actual experiences. Thus, one day Amos was watching a part of the city wall being measured for its straightness by a plumb line, a cord with a weight on the end of it. Then came the voice of the Lord to Amos:

> Behold, I am setting a plumb line
> in the midst of my people Israel;
> I will never again pass by them.
> —Amos 7:8

Put yourself, if you can, in the place of those who listened to Amos. If you were successful and your nation were at its peak of prestige and power, how would you have reacted to these words of judgment spoken by Amos? Amaziah the priest reacted by being thoroughly exasperated. He was fed up. He had enough of Amos' ranting and raving.

One day at Bethel, Amaziah said in effect to Amos: "You visionary, get out of here. Go back to Judah, your own country. There you can prophesy all you want. But don't do it around here anymore. This is the king's sanctuary."

Amos was not the kind of person to let that challenge go unanswered. The gist of his answer was: "I am not a prophet by profession; nor do I belong to that group known as 'the sons of the prophets.' I am just a sheep rancher, and I take care of a few sycamore trees. But the Lord put a finger on me and told me to prophesy here."

JUSTICE AND RIGHTEOUSNESS

Having justified his presence in Israel, he followed this with another forecast of destruction. It is little wonder that Amos has been called the prophet of doom. That he surely was. He foresaw the end of Israel coming certainly and totally. Its destruction would be the inevitable consequence of its unfaithfulness to God. This unfaithfulness demonstrated itself in two ways: in the shallowness of its spiritual devotion to Yahweh and in the lack of its personal morality and social justice. Amos was wise enough to see that these two were inseparably related to each other. A deep God-centered religious faith must issue forth in high moral character and concern for others. By the same token, a worship that has self at its center, regardless of all the trappings, must result in low moral standards and little concern for others. Amos reminded his hearers of this truth in these words:

81

I hate, I despise your feasts,
and I take no delight in your solemn assemblies.
Even though you offer me your burnt offerings and cereal offerings,
I will not accept them,
and the peace offerings of your fatted beasts
I will not look upon.
Take away from me the noise of your songs;
to the melody of your harps I will not listen.
But let justice roll down like waters,
and righteousness like an ever-flowing stream.

—Amos 5:21–24

Justice did roll down on Israel. Before half a century passed by, the words of Amos were to ring painfully in Israelite ears as their weary feet walked many a sorrowing mile, at the heels of their captors, into exile.

HOSEA

When we come to the prophet Hosea, we see him as one who was just as much disturbed at the condition of his nation as was Amos. Hosea was active near the end of the reign of Jeroboam, probably continuing through the troubled times that followed it. His concern over the diseased society that was Israel can be seen through the greater part of his book. The following is representative:

Hear the word of the Lord, O
people of Israel;
for the Lord has a controversy
with the inhabitants of the land.
There is no faithfulness or kindness,
and no knowledge of God in the land;
there is swearing, lying, killing,
stealing, and committing adultery;
they break all bounds and murder
follows murder.

—Hosea 4:1–2

A PAINFUL RELATIONSHIP

There is no need to catalog the abuses denounced by Hosea. We would find them to be the same ones that appalled Amos. However, in the story that surrounds Hosea we find a new element. That element has to do with a deep and painful personal experience. Hosea married a woman by the name of Gomer. To their marriage were born three children, two sons and a daughter. This should have been a fine and happy family situation. Such was not the case. Gomer became attracted to other men. She became an adulteress, willing to satisfy the pleasures of those who would pay her keep. This situation pained Hosea deeply. As he thought of the children who had been born to them and as he recalled Gomer's unfaithfulness, he thought also of Israel and Israel's unfaithfulness to God.

So, in bitter heartbreak he said of the first child: "Call his name Jezreel; for yet a little while, and I will punish the house of Jehu for the blood of Jezreel, and I will put an end to the kingdom of the house of Israel."

Of the second child he said: "Call her name Not Pitied, for I will no more have pity on the house of Israel, to forgive them at all."

And of the third child he said: "Call his name Not My People, for you are not my people and I am not your God." (See Hosea 1:4, 6, 9.)

Hosea thus likened his wife's disloyalty to him to Israel's disloyalty to God. Even as Gomer had broken their marriage covenant of love, so had Israel broken the covenant God had made with this nation in the wilderness. In words both beautiful and tender, Hosea reminds Israel of the covenant that God had made at the beginning of its national life:

> When Israel was a child, I loved him,
>   and out of Egypt I called my son.
> The more I called them,
>   the more they went from me;
> they kept sacrificing to the Baals,
>   and burning incense to idols.
>
> Yet it was I who taught Ephraim to walk,
>   I took them up in my arms;
>   but they did not know that I healed them.
> I led them with cords of compassion,
>   with the bands of love,
> and I became to them as one
>   who eases the yoke on their jaws,
>   and I bent down to them and fed them.
>   —Hosea 11:1–4

Then, in a heartrending cry, Hosea expresses the Divine judgment that will surely visit Israel (called also Ephraim by the prophet): "How can I give you up, O Ephraim! / How can I hand you over, O Israel! [Hos. 11:8]"

FORGIVENESS, HOPE, LOVE

If we were now considering the prophet Amos, this would be the end of our story. Israel was simply doomed to destruction. But the story of Hosea does not end here. His love for Gomer was deep and complete. So he sought her out, bought her back from the one who "owned" her, and took her back home to be his wife. He both forgave and redeemed her.

Under the impact of this experience with his own wife, Hosea thought of God and Israel. But this time his words were not bitter; they were filled with hope and love: hope that Israel might yet be saved, and love because he knew how greatly Israel was loved by God. At this time the word of the Lord speaks through him in what is one of the finest insights of the Old Testament:

> "I will betroth you to me in righteousness and in justice, in steadfast love, and in mercy. I will betroth you to me in faithfulness; and you shall know the Lord.
> "And in that day, says the Lord,
> I will answer the heavens
> and they shall answer the earth;
> and the earth shall answer the grain, the wine, and the oil,
> and they shall answer Jezreel;
> and I will sow him for myself in the land.
> And I will have pity on Not pitied,
> and I will say to Not my people, 'You are my people';
> and he shall say, 'Thou art my God.'"
>
> —Hosea 2:19–23

Both Amos and Hosea were concerned chiefly for the conditions of society that they observed in Israel, the Northern Kingdom. When they prophesied the doom of Israel, it was the Northern Kingdom they had in mind. It did not take long for their prophecy to find fulfillment. In the year 722 B.C. Samaria was conquered by the armies of Shalmaneser V of Assyria, and the people of Israel were carried into exile in the distant provinces of the Assyrian empire. In the midst of this upheaval, the Southern Kingdom of Judah remained intact.

ISAIAH

A giant among giants is the best way to describe Isaiah among the prophets of Israel. Not only do we have more of his words recorded than we have from most other Old Testament prophets, but through his words we have the portrayal of a striking and dominant personality. Unlike other prophets, Isaiah moved within the court circle. Having been born into a rich and aristocratic family, he came into association with the leading persons of his society. Yet he was more than a mere product of his environment. Even when he spoke words of judgment, no one dared to silence him. In Isaiah we have the unusual spectacle of a court prophet who was not a yes-man. His call to be a prophet of God is described in chapter 6 of the book that bears his name.

A SPIRITUAL EXPERIENCE

The year was 742 B.C. Great King Uzziah, who had ruled Judah for forty-two years, was dead. As rulers went, King Uzziah was not a bad king. He had tried to do what was right in the sight of God. Nevertheless his own

84

example did little to turn the hearts of the people toward what was right. What would happen now that he was dead? Would Judah be thrown into even greater turmoil? Would conditions get even worse? One can imagine that these questions ran through the mind of Isaiah when he went into the temple to pray, to think, and to meditate. It was in such a period that his autobiography begins with a soul-searching experience.

> In the year that King Uzziah died I saw the Lord sitting upon a throne, high and lifted up; and his train filled the temple. Above him stood the seraphim; each had six wings: with two he covered his face, and with two he covered his feet, and with two he flew. And one called to another and said:
> "Holy, holy, holy is the Lord of hosts;
> the whole earth is full of his glory."
> And the foundations of the thresholds shook at the voice of him who called, and the house was filled with smoke.
> —Isaiah 6:1–4

In the language of picturesque symbolism, Isaiah tells of his being overwhelmed by the majesty and the glory of God. He is bowed down by the vision of the splendor and the holiness of the Almighty. Face to face with the Holy One, he is awed into silence, the silence of reverent wonder. The silence lasts for but a moment. Quickly it is shattered by a cry: "And I said: 'Woe is me! For I am lost; for I am a man of unclean lips, and I dwell in the midst of a people of unclean lips; for my eyes have seen the King, the Lord of hosts! [Isa. 6:5].'"

Before the glory and the righteousness of the Holy One, Isaiah felt himself to be utterly unworthy and unclean. He saw himself as part of a nation that was unworthy and unclean. His cry was a cry of spiritual agony, both for his own plight and the plight of his people. At this point we see the difference between Isaiah and the prophets who came before him. Amos had thundered God's judgment against Israel for *its* sin. Hosea, through his personal experience with a faithless wife, came to an even deeper appreciation of Israel's sin, but it was still *its* sin. When we come to Isaiah, we see in him one who feels himself personally involved in the sin of his people and one who acknowledges that he too is unclean. Isaiah could therefore speak God's word against the sin of his nation as something more than a spectator watching from afar. He could prophesy as one who knew that he himself stood under the judgment of God. "Then flew one of the seraphim to me, having in his hand a burning coal which he had taken with tongs from the altar. And he touched my mouth, and said: 'Behold, this has touched your lips; your guilt is taken away, and your sin forgiven [Isa. 6:6–7].'"

Great was his sense of shame and unworthiness, but much greater was the forgiveness of the Almighty. In the symbolism of the burning coal touching his lips, he bears witness to the forgiving love of God for the repentant sinner. In his proclamations, Isaiah has much to say about the holiness of God and the demands of God. His own experience, however, tells us that Isaiah knew also something of the love and concern of God for this people. This experience of cleansing becomes a turning point in his own life. His testimony (Isaiah 6:8) is: "And I heard the voice of the Lord saying, 'Whom shall I send, and who will go for us?' Then I said, 'Here I am! Send me.'"

The wonderful experience of forgiveness, of being right with God, is followed by a call to action. Here are people stumbling over their own sins. Here are people who have veered so far away from the law of the Lord that they no longer know what is right and what is wrong. Here are people heading toward national disaster. Who will go to them and speak the word they need to hear? Who will be the mouth of the Lord to them? "Here I am!" answered Isaiah. "Send me."

Parable of a Vineyard

As we read the words of this great prophet, as we see him moving serenely and stately through the various crises that confront Judah, we know without a doubt that here was one sent from God. One exquisite piece of writing—the parable of the vineyard—exemplifies his art. This parable sums up a major portion of Isaiah's message to his people: God's hope for Judah, Judah's unfaithful stewardship, and the inescapable consequence of disaster. In words at first tender and then menacing, he speaks of his beloved nation.

> Let me sing for my beloved
>   a love song concerning his vineyard:
> My beloved had a vineyard
>   on a very fertile hill.
> He digged it and cleared it of stones,
>   and planted it with choice vines;
> he built a watchtower in the midst of it,
>   and hewed out a wine vat in it,
> and he looked for it to yield grapes,
>   but it yielded wild grapes.
>
> And now, O inhabitants of Jerusalem
>   and men of Judah,
> judge, I pray you, between me
>   and my vineyard.
> What more was there to do for my vineyard,
>   that I have not done in it?
> When I looked for it to yield grapes,
>   why did it yield wild grapes?

And now I will tell you
  what I will do to my vineyard.
I will remove its hedge,
  and it shall be devoured;
I will break down its wall
  and it shall be trampled down.
I will make it a waste;
  it shall not be pruned or hoed,
  and briers and thorns shall grow up;
I will also command the clouds
  that they rain no rain upon it.

For the vineyard of the Lord of hosts
  is the house of Israel,
and the men of Judah
  are his pleasant planting;
and he looked for justice,
  but behold, bloodshed;
for righteousness,
  but behold, a cry!

—Isaiah 5:1-7

THREE CRISES

On three separate occasions during the lifetime of Isaiah it looked as if the threats against Judah in the above parable would be realized. In 734 B.C. Syria and Israel conspired against Judah and arrayed themselves against Jerusalem. When Ahaz and his court heard of this, they were overcome with fear. So afraid were they that the scripture says of them that their hearts "shook as the trees of the forest shake before the wind." Isaiah, who is found in the middle of the crisis, goes to meet Ahaz and tells him not to worry about "these two smoldering stumps of firebrands," referring to Rezin, king of Syria, and Pekah, king of Israel. To bolster the king's confidence, Isaiah tells Ahaz to ask for a sign. Ahaz refuses, but Isaiah gives him one anyway. He tells him that a young maiden will give birth to a son and will call his name "Immanuel," meaning "God is with us." The reason she will give her son that name is because God will deliver Judah from both the kings that now oppress it.

But Ahaz refused to take encouragement from Isaiah. Instead, he sent emissaries to see Tiglath-pileser, king of Assyria, and emptied the temple treasury for tribute to him, asking him to come and help. When Rezin and Pekah heard of Judah's alliance with Assyria, they dropped their siege of Jerusalem and headed home. Meanwhile the armies of Assyria marched on Damascus, the capital of Syria, and conquered it. It was not long before Samaria also fell.

In 711 B.C. Judah feared attack by Assyria and sent messengers to Egypt in order to rally support. To Isaiah, this was a further sign of Judah's lack of confidence in God. When attack did come, for some reason Sargon II, king of Assyria, bypassed Jerusalem but destroyed Ashdod, a city of the Philistines on the Mediterranean coast.

During the life of Isaiah, the most important political crisis came in the year 701 B.C. In that year Sennacherib, king of Assyria, invaded Judah, conquering one fortified city after another. Finally he sent his principal envoy to Jerusalem, demanding its surrender. Knowing that the people were hungry, thirsty, tired, and discouraged, he spoke loudly to the Jerusalem diplomats that came to meet him outside the walls of the city. He painted a beautiful word picture of how fine everything would be for the people if they surrendered: "Every one of you will eat of his own vine, and every one of his own fig tree, and every one of you will drink the water of his own cistern [Isa. 36:16]."

With such a grave situation facing him, King Hezekiah sent his servants to Isaiah to ask of him a word from the Lord. Isaiah assured him that the city would be saved and that circumstances would force Sennacherib to return to his own country. As it turned out, the city was spared and the Assyrian army did leave. It should be pointed out, however, that this story, which we find in chapters 36 and 37 of the book of Isaiah, is told also more fully and probably more accurately in 2 Kings 18—19. The latter account tells that King Hezekiah paid tribute to Sennacherib in order to save Jerusalem, suggesting that he did not put very much faith in the word of the Lord that came to him through Isaiah. At any rate, Jerusalem still stood. The people still felt confident that God was with them, regardless of how they were living.

This was a shallow kind of confidence, since it was not based on deep spiritual devotion or moral uprightness. Isaiah knew this, just as he knew that doom would some day overtake the people for their infidelity. It would be a destruction that would be sure and complete. He warned: "Destruction is decreed, overflowing with righteousness. For the Lord, the Lord of hosts, will make a full end, as decreed, in the midst of all the earth [Isa. 10:22-23]."

EVIDENCES OF HOPE

Yet even as he spoke of complete destruction, he was not without hope. This hope showed itself in the conviction that a *remnant* would be saved, that a few would survive the awful days to come. In this remnant lay the future hope of Israel. "In that day the remnant of Israel and the survivors of the house of Jacob will no more lean upon him that smote them, but will lean upon the Lord, the Holy One of Israel, in truth. A remnant will return, the remnant of Jacob, to the mighty God [Isa. 10:20-21]."

The idea of the remnant is not the only evidence of hope to be found in Isaiah. We see it plainly and magnificently in two outstanding passages, Isaiah 9:2-7 and 11:1-9. These passages appear to have been written by Isaiah on the occasion of the coronation of a king, perhaps King Hezekiah. Each passage embodies the hope that the king, whose coronation was being celebrated, would in truth be "the Lord's Messiah." The fact that Hezekiah, or any other earthly ruler known to the people, was not this great Messiah for whom they hoped did not dim their ardor. If anything, it only increased it. They looked ever to the future for the one who would be for them "Wonderful Counselor, Mighty God, Everlasting Father, Prince of Peace." As Christians, we believe that this one has come in the person of Jesus Christ. So when we read either of these passages, we associate them with Christ.

The holiness of God, faith in the working out of God's purposes, and a great hope that after the destruction a remnant would return—these are some of the major themes of Isaiah, a giant among the prophets.

MICAH

If we compare by volume the literary output of the prophets, we see that the book of Micah is only seven chapters long. Of that, almost three full chapters probably did not come from him. However, the quantitative standard is no reliable standard by which to judge the quality of the contributions of the prophets. This is particularly true in Micah's case. In a way less spectacular than Isaiah, his contemporary, he made an important impact on the moral and spiritual climate of his day. Jeremiah, in his time, reported that the "elders of the land" gave Micah credit for much of the religious reform instituted by King Hezekiah late in the eighth century B.C. Unlike Isaiah the city aristocrat, Micah was a humble laborer from Moresheth, an obscure village twenty-five miles southwest of Jerusalem. He knew from firsthand experience the hard lot of the working people and of the poor of the land. He knew also how they were oppressed by the well-to-do. This concern for the laboring class and their unfair treatment at the hands of the rich is reflected in the words that he spoke in the name of the Lord.

> They covet fields, and seize them;
> and houses, and take them away;
> they oppress a man and his house,
> a man and his inheritance.

> The women of my people you drive out
> from their pleasant houses;
> from their young children you take away
> my glory forever.

And I said:
hear, you heads of Jacob
   and rulers of the house of Israel!
Is it not for you to know justice?—
   you who hate the good and love the evil
who tear the skin from off my people,
   and their flesh from off their bones.
                              —Micah 2:2, 9; 3:1-2

The book of Micah sums up the duty of persons, both in relation to God and in relation to one another. It sums up the duty of a nation that is faithful to its covenant pledge. Empty religious practices are contrasted with sincere religious living in these ringing words:

"With what shall I come before the Lord,
   and bow myself before God on high?
Shall I come before him with burnt offerings,
   with calves a year old?
Will the Lord be pleased with thousands of rams,
   with ten thousands of rivers of oil?
Shall I give my first-born for my transgression,
   the fruit of my body for the sin of my soul?"
He has showed you, O man, what is good;
   and what does the Lord require of you
but to do justice, and to love kindness,
   and to walk humbly with your God?
                              —Micah 6:6-8

JOSIAH AND THE LAST DAYS OF JUDAH

To understand the life and work of Jeremiah, some appreciation is needed of the times in which he lived. He must have been born during the reign of King Josiah, who ruled Judah from 640–609 B.C. The D editor holds an extremely high estimate of Josiah, for it was under him that the great Deuteronomic reforms took place. These reforms were occasioned by the finding of a book, called the book of the covenant, in the temple by a certain Hilkiah, the high priest. This book of the covenant probably comprised the heart of the present book of Deuteronomy, notably chapters 12—26. The supposed author of the book of the covenant was Moses, though actually it was written by another hand probably during the seventh century B.C. in the reign of Manasseh, a king of Judah. This book was a reaction to the immoral and idolatrous practices that filled the land while he was king.

When Josiah heard the contents of the book of the covenant, he "rent his clothes"; that is, he tore them to pieces as a sign of mourning and repentance. Immediately he set in motion a series of religious reforms as suggested by the book. He threw out all the idols that had been in the temple of Yahweh; deposed their priests; destroyed the houses of the cult prostitutes; broke down the altars of all the high places; and, as far as he was able, did away with all vestiges of corrupt worship practices throughout the land. True to the Deuteronomic idea, he centered the worship of God at the temple in Jerusalem. So impressed by his actions was the later D editor, that he wrote of him: "Before him there was no king like him, who turned to the Lord with all his heart and with all his soul and with all his might, according to all the law of Moses; nor did any like him arise after him [2 Kings 23:25]."

Josiah met his death at the hand of Pharaoh Neco, who was on his way to help Assyria against the forces of Babylon. Jehoahaz ruled in his stead, but that lasted only three months. When Pharaoh Neco returned from his trip to Mesopotamia, he deposed Jehoahaz and put on the throne Jehoiakim, another son of Josiah. Jehoiakim reigned for eleven years (609–598 B.C.). It was during his reign that Jeremiah first began his prophetic ministry. In 598 B.C. during the first invasion of the Babylonians, Jehoiakim died and his son Jehoiachin succeeded him. He ruled only three months before he surrendered to the Babylonian army surrounding Jerusalem. He and the queen mother, along with thousands of others, were taken away into exile. Zedekiah, Jehoiachin's uncle, was appointed king by Nebuchadrezzar.* For ten years he remained friendly to Babylon. In the ninth year of his reign he let himself be swayed by the pro-Egyptian party in Jerusalem and refused to pay any further tribute to Babylon. This proved to be a serious mistake.

Nebuchadrezzar sent his commanders against Jerusalem. After a year and a half they captured the city in 587 B.C., burning most of it including the palace and the temple. They caught up with Zedekiah and his soldiers who had fled the city in the hope of regrouping their forces. Zedekiah's own sons were killed as he looked on, his eyes were put out, and he was bound and carried off to Babylon. This defeat at the hand of the Babylonians marked the end of the kingdom of Judah. Gedaliah was appointed to govern the affairs of the desolated country and set up headquarters at Mizpah, north of Jerusalem. He governed for five years before he was assassinated by a certain Ishmael. The latter fled safely to the land of Moab. Those notables who had been left in the land feared reprisal from Babylon for the killing of Gedaliah, although they had no hand in it. As quickly as they could, they fled to Egypt, taking an unwilling Jeremiah with them. Such was the turbulent history of the period in which Jeremiah, one of the greatest of the prophets, lived and prophesied.

God Calls Jeremiah

Born into a family of priests about 628 B.C., Jeremiah grew up in the little town of Anathoth, two miles northeast of Jerusalem. There is no reason to

*This is believed by many to be a more accurate spelling of the name of the king commonly known as Nebuchadnezzar.

believe that Jeremiah ever served as a priest himself. He received his call to the prophetic ministry when still a young man. This call made a deep and lasting impression on his life, as his own testimony in the first chapter of his book tells us. It was not a call that he accepted easily. In this respect, he reminds us of Moses. Yet so firmly was God's hand on him, that he could not resist. As he looked back upon his call from the perspective of his ministry, it seemed to him that this must have been God's intention for him even before he was born. His words are:

> Now the word of the Lord came to me saying,
>> "Before I formed you in the womb
>> I knew you,
>> and before you were born I consecrated you;
>> I appointed you a prophet to the
>> nations."
>
> Then I said, "Ah, Lord God! Behold, I do not know how to speak, for I am only a youth." But the Lord said to me,
>> "Do not say, 'I am only a youth';
>> for to all to whom I send you you
>> shall go,
>> and whatever I command you you
>> shall speak.
>> Be not afraid of them,
>> for I am with you to deliver you,
>> says the Lord."
>
> Then the Lord put forth his hand and touched my mouth; and the Lord said to me,
>> "Behold, I have put my words in your
>> mouth.
>> See, I have set you this day over
>> nations and over kingdoms,
>> to pluck up and to break down,
>> to destroy and to overthrow,
>> to build and to plant."
>
> —Jeremiah 1:4–10

JEREMIAH'S PERSONAL TRIALS

God had called Jeremiah. The prophet's only peace could be in the service of his Lord. But this acceptance of his summons did not mean idyllic bliss for the prophet. On the contrary, speaking the word of the Lord kept Jeremiah in continual hot water with the authorities. Twice he was beaten and three times he was imprisoned for his verbal attacks. Once he was thrown down an old abandoned well and left to rot in the mire. Only the intervention of a prominent Ethiopian by the name of Ebed-melech saved him from certain death. Finally near the end of his life he was taken against his will to Egypt. In all likelihood he met a martyr's death at the hands of the Jews, against whom he continued to prophesy.

92

There are people who are able to bear up under great personal abuse. They are strong personalities, able to take things in their stride. But Jeremiah was not one of these. His was a sensitive spirit. He felt very deeply the antagonisms that were leveled against him by his own people. He sincerely wanted the goodwill of his fellow Israelites, not their scorn. He hated it when he had to prophesy destruction against them, when he had to chastise them for their immoralities and unfaithfulness. He hated it because he knew they would hate him for it. Yet he had no choice. He was under a commission from God. He was a spokesman for the Lord and what the Lord gave him to speak, that he had to speak! His soul-searching struggle is evident from his personal confessions:

> O Lord, thou hast deceived me,
>   and I was deceived;
> thou art stronger than I,
>   and thou hast prevailed.
> I have become a laughingstock all the day;
>   every one mocks me.
> For whenever I speak, I cry out,
>   I shout, "Violence and destruction!"
> For the word of the Lord has become for me
>   a reproach and derision all day long.
> If I say, "I will not mention him,
>   or speak any more in his name,"
> there is in my heart as it were a burning fire
>   shut up in my bones,
> and I am weary with holding it in,
>   and I cannot.
> —Jeremiah 20:7–9

A WORD OF JUDGMENT

Whatever it may have cost him in personal discomfort, Jeremiah related the judgment of God to conditions as he saw them in the nation of his day. He rebuked the people for their unfaithfulness to Yahweh and for their worship of other gods:

> For my people have committed two evils:
>   they have forsaken me,
> the fountain of living waters,
>   and hewed out cisterns for themselves,
> broken cisterns,
>   that can hold no water.
> —Jeremiah 2:13

He lashed out against false priests and false prophets who soothed the people with syrupy words, who shouted "Peace, peace," when there was no peace. He accused those in places of influence of practicing injustices, oppressing the aliens in their midst, taking advantage of the fatherless and the widows, and "shedding innocent blood." To everyone who would listen, he pointed out the contrast between their worship at the temple and the corrupt way in which they lived. Not even the kings of Judah were spared his tirades in behalf of righteousness. When King Zedekiah toyed with the idea of an alliance with Egypt, Jeremiah put around his neck a yoke worn by oxen, symbolizing the yoke of Babylon that Judah was now under. If Judah should refuse to stay under this yoke, Jeremiah was saying, her doom would be swift and sure.

So far gone was his people's ability to distinguish right from wrong, that Jeremiah could say:

> Can the Ethiopian change his skin
> or the leopard his spots?
> Then also you can do good
> who are accustomed to do evil.
> —Jeremiah 13:23

Jeremiah had no alternative but to prophesy the destruction of his nation, because at every turn he saw that which invited it. Therefore, as the Lord's spokesman, he was compelled to thunder: "Thus says the Lord of hosts: So will I break this people and this city, as one breaks a potter's vessel, so that it can never be mended [Jer. 19:10]."

A WORD OF HOPE

Yet Jeremiah was not without a word of hope for his people. Jerusalem would be destroyed and the country devastated; men, women, and children would be carried into exile. Nevertheless, all was not lost. He had a strong hope in the future. Even while the armies of Nebuchadrezzar were besieging Jerusalem, he contracted to buy a plot of ground in Anathoth from a relative. After the fall of Jerusalem, when Gedaliah was governor, he sought to cheer up the exiles by assuring them that they would return to their own land one day.

It is when we consider the covenant in Jeremiah that we come to one of the most significant parts of the Old Testament. The prophet was aware of a time when Israel had been true to the covenant:

> I remember the devotion of your youth,
> your love as a bride,
> how you followed me in the wilderness,
> in a land not sown.
> Israel was holy to the Lord,
> the first fruits of his harvest.
> —Jeremiah 2:2-3

A New Covenant

Jeremiah was aware of how blatantly Israel had broken the covenant, of how it lived in complete disregard of it. In the eleventh chapter of Jeremiah, which seems to combine the thoughts of Jeremiah and the editing of the Deuteronomist, this stinging indictment is made:

> They have gone after other gods to serve them; the house of Israel and the house of Judah have broken my covenant which I made with their fathers. Therefore, thus says the Lord, Behold, I am bringing evil upon them which they cannot escape; though they cry to me, I will not listen to them.
>
> —Jeremiah 11:10-11

Jeremiah must have pondered long and hard the troublesome question of why his people did not keep their covenant promise. Why was the keeping of God's law not important to them? Why did they not obey Yahweh? Slowly and painstakingly the answer came. It was a matter of the heart. Their sin was engraved on the tablet of their heart with the point of a diamond. It was really a question of their innermost motives. Judah *did not want* to keep the law of Yahweh. The people had no real *inward desire* to obey. They did not need a new law, the will of God had been made plain enough. What they did need was a new motive that would impel them from within to be faithful and to obey the holy covenant of love and righteousness. What was needed in this hour was an operation on the hearts of people. We can be eternally grateful to the editor, whoever he was, who preserved for us these key thoughts of Jeremiah in the following inspiring words:

> Behold, the days are coming, says the Lord, when I will make a new covenant with the house of Israel and the house of Judah, not like the covenant which I made with their fathers when I took them by the hand to bring them out of the land of Egypt, my covenant which they broke, though 1 was their husband, says the Lord. But this is the covenant which I will make with the house of Israel after those days, says the Lord: I will put my law within them, and I will write it upon their hearts; and I will be their God, and they shall be my people. And no longer shall each man teach his neighbor and each his brother, saying, "Know the Lord," for they shall all know me, from the least of them to the greatest, says the Lord; for I will forgive their iniquity, and I will remember their sin no more.
>
> —Jeremiah 31:31-34

With this we close the curtain on the life of Jeremiah and on the lives of those other prophets of God who preceded him. As we do so, we stand in awe of the time that produced persons of such spiritual stature. In them-

95

selves, they carried the covenant promise of Israel. This was a time when giants walked the earth.

Scene 4.
FEARS, TEARS, AND HOPE
(Ezekiel, Job, and Second Isaiah)

EXILE

It is a time-honored truth that out of adversity can come greatness. Such was certainly the case with Israel (meaning now the entire nation including both the Northern Kingdom and the Southern Kingdom). The sixth century B.C. was a time of adversity for Israel. On three separate occasions inhabitants of Judah and Jerusalem were taken into exile in Babylonia. Those taken were the princes, nobles, priests, chief artisans, and the like. Only the poor of the land remained that they might till the soil. If the account of Jeremiah is correct, it would seem that some 4,600 persons were driven into exile. In terms of an entire nation or even a city such as Jerusalem, this is not a large number. However, since it was the leaders who were taken away, the country was left without the services of those who had formerly directed its national destiny. And Jerusalem itself had been sacked and burned. Since a country is symbolized by those who are its leaders, it must have seemed to the people of that time that Israel itself had been driven into exile.

One does not need a vivid imagination to guess the feelings of despair and hopelessness that must have overwhelmed those exiles who trod mile after weary mile toward a strange land. Nor was the despair of the Israelites any less once they had settled in the nation of the enemy. To be sure, many of those who had been carried away were able to adjust to their new surroundings. There is no reason to believe that their captors were particularly cruel to them. There is ample evidence to show that the exiles enjoyed a certain amount of freedom. Many were given land to farm and houses to live in. They were even permitted the right of gathering together in assembly. Some became traders and established lucrative business ventures.

HARD QUESTIONS

But to the sensitive Israelite there were many plaguing questions, questions that arose by virtue of their separation from their native land and from their beloved Jerusalem. When they thought of God, it was as God of the land of Israel. How, then could they worship God in a land that was not theirs? They were aware that Israel had sinned against God. But did

Israel deserve such terrible punishment at God's hands? Compared with other nations, Israel was far more righteous. Why, then, must it suffer so? Indeed, why must some suffer more than others? Finally, what was to be the future of the Israelites? They had been told by their prophets that they were God's chosen people. Was this now the end? Or did a greater destiny yet await them? Such were the questions that must have troubled many of the exiles. The deep despair felt by many of the Israelites is mirrored in Psalm 137:1-6.

> By the waters of Babylon,
>   there we sat down and wept,
>   when we remembered Zion.
> On the willows there
>   we hung up our lyres.
> For there our captors
>   required of us songs,
> and our tormentors, mirth, saying,
>   "Sing us one of the songs of Zion!"
>
> How shall we sing the Lord's song
>   in a foreign land?
> If I forget you, O Jerusalem,
>   let my right hand wither!
> Let my tongue cleave to the roof of my mouth,
>   if I do not remember you,
> if I do not set Jerusalem
>   above my highest joy!

If there were questions in this time of adversity for Israel, there were also those whom God raised up to give answers—those who spoke for God to the people. Through them Israel was led to see the nature of its destiny and to discover God's purpose for it.

EZEKIEL

"Ezekiel saw the wheel, way up in the middle of the air"—so run the words of a beloved spiritual. The reference is to the vision that constituted Ezekiel's call to be a prophet of the Lord. A contemporary of Jeremiah, Ezekiel was one of the persons carried away into exile after the Babylonian invasion of 598 B.C. It appears that his call to be a prophet came about five years later, while he lived in exile. The vision of the throne-topped chariot recorded in Ezekiel 1:1-28 became for the prophet a deeply moving experience of the glory of God and of God's call to him to "speak to the house of Israel." Under the compulsion of that experience, Ezekiel did speak for God to his nation. His words were of two kinds: words of judgment and words of promise.

JUDGMENT

The words of judgment that he spoke came before the fall of Jerusalem in 587 B.C. He lashed out against his people for their worship of idols and for their alliances with foreign nations. Both of these practices, in Ezekiel's view, were perversions indicating a lack of faith in God. As a predictor of destruction because of the people's sin, he followed squarely in the footsteps of the earlier prophets. Like Jeremiah, he used not only words but actions to portray vividly the fate that awaited an erring people. On one occasion he packed up his things and in the sight of the people carried them out as if he were going into exile. This was to be a sign to them.

> In the morning the word of the Lord came to me: "Son of man, has not the house of Israel, the rebellious house, said to you, 'What are you doing?' Say to them, 'Thus says the Lord God: This oracle concerns the prince in Jerusalem and all the house of Israel who are in it.' Say, 'I am a sign for you: as I have done, so shall it be done to them; they shall go into exile, into captivity.'"
>
> —Ezekiel 12:8–11

PROMISE AND HOPE

Sometime after the destruction of Jerusalem in 587, the tone of Ezekiel's message changed. He spoke then to a despairing and heavyhearted people in exile. They were suffering from being cut off from the land of their birth. And they were filled with questions. To these the prophet brought a word of hope, a word of promise. The closing chapters of his book look forward to a time when those in exile would return to Israel and to a time when the temple in Jerusalem would be restored. In minute detail he outlined the measurements of the temple and the duties of the priests who would function there. He envisioned that the temple would be at the very heart of the restored nation of Israel, and that the priests would interpret to the people God's will for them in their community life. To the temple, and so to the midst of Israel, the glory of the Lord would return, prophesied Ezekiel. Compared to ideas of Israel's destiny which were found in the other prophets, Ezekiel's ideas seem to us rather narrow and confining. Nevertheless he does point the people to something central that had been previously corrupted: the worship of and obedience to the one God.

Perhaps the most familiar of Ezekiel's words of promise are those recorded in chapter 37 of the book that bears his name. In a vision he saw himself in a valley filled with bones. "Son of man, can these bones live?" asks the Lord. To which Ezekiel answers, "Thou knowest, Lord." As Ezekiel continues to behold the vision, a rattling is heard as the bones begin to knit together and to take on sinew and flesh and skin. Then the Lord breathes the breath of life into them, and they stand erect upon their feet! Then the voice of the Lord speaks again:

> Son of man, these bones are the whole house of Israel. . . . Behold, I will open your graves, and raise you from your graves, O my people; and I will bring you home into the land of Israel. . . . And I will put my Spirit within you, and you shall live, and I will place you in your own land; then you shall know that I, the Lord, have spoken, and I have done it, says the Lord.
>
> —Ezekiel 37:11–12, 14

There is much in the book of Ezekiel that cannot possibly be attributed to the prophet because the style, thought, and circumstances are so different from the rest of his message. We can only conclude that these other ideas in the book come from one, unknown to us, who may have been a disciple of Ezekiel. Much later than Ezekiel's lifetime, he combined his own thought with that of the prophet. In this anonymous editor, we see one who looked for a messianic king after the fashion of David (Ezekiel 34:23); who spoke of the "new heart I will give you, and a new spirit I will put within you [Ezek. 36:26]"; and who announced the "covenant of peace [Ezek. 34:25]" God made with Israel. There was, therefore, in the words of Ezekiel much to lift up faint hearts.

JOB

Why must people suffer so? Why has God treated some persons in such ways? These were burning questions of the sixth century B.C. A poet whose name we do not know, but whose work must rank with the greatest of the world's literature, used the problem of suffering as a starting point. This is the concern that meets us at the beginning of the book of Job. The poet was acquainted with the tale of a wealthy Edomite rancher, and he used it as the setting for a deep discussion about the meaning of life. Job was the name of the rancher in the story. He had everything any man could want—wealth, a fine family, a good reputation in the community, excellent health, and loyal servants to attend him. In addition, he was a very religious and devout man. Then tragedy struck. He lost all his wealth, his sons and daughters were killed in a violent windstorm, and he himself was afflicted with sores over his whole body. His situation was one of sheer desperation. So loathsome was his plight that death would have seemed sweet by comparison. In bitter words, Job beat on heaven's door:

> Let the day perish wherein I was born,
>   and the night which said,
> "A man-child is conceived."

> Let that day be darkness!
>> May God above not seek it,
>> nor light shine upon it.
>
> Let the stars of its dawn be dark;
>> let it hope for light, but have none,
>> nor see the eyelids of the morning;
> because it did not shut the doors of my mother's womb,
>> nor hide trouble from my eyes.
>
>> —Job 3:3, 9–10

The case of Job, the righteous man who had to suffer, seems extreme. Nevertheless those who know suffering from firsthand experience can easily feel a close kinship with the central figure of the poet's discourses. For he too wanted to know the reason for suffering.

Yet Job learned something far greater than the answer to the question of suffering. What the poet was really speaking of was a person's relationship to God. Just what is a person to do when the whole world comes crashing down? Where does one turn? This must have been the thought of many a Hebrew in the sixth century B.C. The poet's answer? One turns to God in complete and unconditional surrender. In other words, a person gives oneself to God in a response that the New Testament describes as faith.

This is what Job did. Confronted by the majesty and the power and the wisdom of the Almighty, Job saw how little he was, how petty were his thoughts, and how small were his questions. In awe before his Maker, he bowed down in adoration and repentance. His religion had been secondhand; now he had come to know firsthand the God who is God.

> I had heard of thee by the hearing of the ear,
>> but now my eye sees thee;
> therefore I despise myself,
>> and repent in dust and ashes.
>
>> —Job 42:5–6

The poet of the book of Job, a literary master unexcelled anywhere in the Old Testament, spoke to the needs of troubled souls in a time of personal and social tumult. He endeavored to lead his people to God through surrender and repentance. Only in this way could life have meaning for them.

SECOND ISAIAH

If most of the Jews in exile were confused as to the future and destiny of Israel, there was one spiritual giant who was not. Once again, we do not know his name; we have given him the name of Second Isaiah. His inspiring and exalted words comprise chapters 40—55 in the book of Isaiah. He is not to be confused with the prophet of the eighth century

B.C. who lived in Jerusalem. That was another person altogether. Second Isaiah lived and worked during the period of the exile. His message was for a people who had been conquered and disillusioned, and who wondered what the future held. To their wondering, he brings an answer.

In language that flows beautifully and is both majestic and joyous, he paints the picture of the coming of the Holy One. God is portrayed as coming to redeem Israel, to restore the covenant with it. Israel will henceforth be God's servant to all the nations, that all may know the God of the whole earth. Thus, his words to Israel open with a song of rejoicing:

> Comfort, comfort my people,
>   says your God.
> Speak tenderly to Jerusalem,
>   and cry to her
> that her warfare is ended,
>   that her iniquity is pardoned.
>   —Isaiah 40:1–2

God will come to defend the nation that has been holy:

> A voice cries:
> "In the wilderness prepare the way of the Lord,
>   make straight in the desert a highway for our God.
> Every valley shall be lifted up,
>   and every mountain and hill be made low;
> the uneven ground shall become level,
>   and the rough places a plain.
> And the glory of the Lord shall be revealed,
>   and all flesh shall see it together,
> for the mouth of the Lord has spoken."
>   —Isaiah 40:3–5

God will redeem Israel, for God alone is its Savior. Let there be great joy and rejoicing in the land:

> Awake, awake,
>   put on your strength, O Zion;
> put on your beautiful garments,
>   O Jerusalem, the holy city. . . .
>
> How beautiful upon the mountains
>   are the feet of him who brings good tidings,
> who publishes peace, who brings good tidings of good,
>   who publishes salvation,
>   who says to Zion, "Your God reigns."
> Hark, your watchmen lift up their voice,
>   together they sing for joy;
> for eye to eye they see
>   the return of the Lord to Zion.

Break forth together into singing,
  you waste places of Jerusalem;
for the Lord has comforted his people,
  he has redeemed Jerusalem.
The Lord has bared his holy arm
  before the eyes of all the nations;
and all the ends of the earth shall see
  the salvation of our God.

—Isaiah 52:1, 7–10

"Servant of the Lord"

But not only will God redeem Israel. Israel is to be the servant of the Lord
for the redemption of *all* the nations. The purpose of God has now a grand
and universal design, a design echoed in these words of the prophet:

Behold my servant, whom I uphold,
  my chosen, in whom my soul delights;
I have put my spirit upon him,
  he will bring forth justice to the nations.

I am the Lord, I have called you in righteousness,
  I have taken you by the hand and kept you;
I have given you as a covenant to the people,
  a light to the nations,
  to open the eyes that are blind,
to bring out the prisoners from the dungeon,
  from the prison those who sit in darkness.

—Isaiah 42:1, 6–7

Why has Israel been chosen to be this servant to the nations? Only God
knows the answer to that question. Out of a great love God chose Israel
and they made covenant together. The terms of the covenant were that
Yahweh would be Israel's God and Israel would be God's people. But, said
the prophet, this election by God carries with it a sense of responsibility.
Ought not Israel feel this responsibility? Has Israel not been a servant
who has suffered at the hands of the Holy One? Has not God's judgment
come upon it for sins that were not Israel's alone? Has Israel not taken on
itself the punishment for the sins of many nations? Chapters 52:13—53:12
picture for us this suffering servant of the Lord as one who suffers on
behalf of others that they might be healed.

To such a role Second Isaiah calls Israel. In this way Israel is to fulfill its
destiny; in this manner it is to be a light to the nations. Thus, referring to
Israel, the prophet pictures this servant:

He was despised and rejected by men;
  a man of sorrows, and acquainted with grief;

102

and as one from whom men hide their faces
he was despised, and we esteemed him not.

Surely he has borne our griefs
and carried our sorrows;
yet we esteemed him stricken,
smitten by God, and afflicted.
But he was wounded for our transgressions,
he was bruised for our iniquities;
upon him was the chastisement that made us whole,
and with his stripes we are healed.

By his knowledge shall the righteous one, my servant,
make many to be accounted righteous.
—Isaiah 53:3–5, 11

A LIGHT TO THE NATIONS

So does Second Isaiah enlarge the scope of the covenant. Formerly, the covenant was the pledge between God and Israel. Here is the great leap. Now the covenant is meant to be a cord binding all nations, for the Holy One of Israel is "the God of the whole earth." Here is a mighty affirmation. Here, indeed, is a new thing. It is little wonder that Second Isaiah has been called Israel's "profoundest thinker." For through him God speaks, saying:

I will give you as a light to the nations,
that my salvation may reach to the end of the earth.
—Isaiah 49:6

We shall soon see how Israel responded to this portrayal of its destiny. With disappointment, we shall see what seems to us a shrinking from the high calling of the *wider* covenant responsibility envisioned for it by Second Isaiah. Further, as we read the words in Isaiah 52:13—53:12, not a nation but a person comes to mind. If the nation of Israel did not fulfill the "suffering servant" role, another came who did. He was one who suffered for the sins of many; yes, for the sins of all the world, that through him the world might be saved. For the Christian, the "suffering servant" is none other than Jesus Christ, the herald of the new covenant. Although this is a jump ahead in our story, we can hardly read these words of Second Isaiah without thinking of the man of Galilee.

The idea of the covenant reached its highest peak in Second Isaiah. The covenant—God's special relationship to a people—was now broadened to include all the nations of the earth. This insight really introduces us to the meaning of covenant as we find it in the New Testament. It forms, as it were, a bridge between the old understanding of the covenant and the new. To Second Isaiah belongs the credit for building that bridge. Before we can walk over it, however, we have still some five hundred years of Jewish history to consider. This period holds much interesting and important information for us; but it will have no insights comparable to those of the period we leave behind us, when the voice of God spoke through prophets with an authority that has seldom been equaled.

Scene 5.

A NEW BEGINNING; SUCCESS, YET FAILURE

(Ezra, Nehemiah, Esther, the Maccabees, Daniel, Jonah, and Ruth)

FREE TO RETURN

In the year 539 B.C. the mighty kingdom of Babylon fell before the onslaught of the armies of Cyrus, king of Persia. This date was a high-water mark in the history of the people of Israel. In 538 B.C. Cyrus issued a decree allowing the Jewish exiles to return to their homeland. One can imagine the tears of joy that must have greeted this edict from the Persian ruler. To be sure, there were many Jews who never would return. They were comfortably settled in Babylon; they had been there for two generations. They had adopted the ways, customs, and in some cases the religion, of the land. Some were quite content to stay. But many others wished to return. They were discontent in a foreign land and harbored a deep, persistent longing to return to the land of their ancestors.

This longing had a religious base. To return to the land of Israel meant, in their minds, to return to the place where God could more rightly be worshiped and served. Israel was linked to Yahweh as was no other land. God's blessing was there. Thus in order to be truly the people of God and to receive God's blessing, they felt they should be in Israel, and even more particularly in Jerusalem, the Holy City. With great rejoicing and with hopes high, the first caravan of Jewish exiles made the long journey from Babylon to Jerusalem. It is with the edict of Cyrus and the arrival of this first group of exiles in Jerusalem that the book of Ezra begins.

EZRA AND NEHEMIAH

Before we go any farther, there are a few things that must be said about the writings of both Ezra and Nehemiah in order to understand the story that they tell. Both of their books were written and edited by a person who is referred to as the Chronicler. He took reports that came from Ezra the scribe and the memoirs of Nehemiah the governor. He then added quite a number of details of his own and put the whole thing together in what we now know as the book of Ezra and the book of Nehemiah.

But that is not all. Somehow in the process of putting together the writings of Ezra and Nehemiah, the Chronicler misplaced certain portions of the story. Unless we realize this, the story gets all mixed up in the reading of it. When we put the events mentioned in Ezra and Nehemiah in chronological order, this is the sequence in which they actually happened:

1. Return of the first exiles to Jerusalem under Sheshbazzar (538 B.C.) and the initial attempt to rebuild the temple; then later the actual rebuilding of the temple under the leadership of Zerubbabel—520–515 B.C. (Ezra 1:1—6:22)
2. Nehemiah receives permission from King Artaxerxes I to go to Jerusalem to rebuild the walls about 445 B.C. He also makes reforms concerning the temple, sabbath, intermarriage. (Nehemiah 1:1—7:73a; Nehemiah 11:1—13:31)
3. Ezra returns with another group of exiles around 442 B.C. His purpose is to introduce the "law" that would regulate the community of Jews and to institute reforms regarding intermarriage. (Ezra 7:1—8:36; Nehemiah 7:73b—8:18; Ezra 9:1—10:44; Nehemiah 9:1—10:39)

Sheshbazzar was the leader of the first group of exiles to take the long journey up the Tigris River, across the top of the Fertile Crescent, and southward into the land of Israel. The journey closely parallels that of some Aramaean clans centuries earlier under the leadership of Abraham. The only thing of note that seems to have been accomplished under Sheshbazzar's leadership was the building of an altar in Jerusalem, on which the people might make their sacrifices and offerings. He also made a start in rebuilding the temple but abandoned the project when Israel's neighbors protested.

ZERUBBABEL AND THE TEMPLE

It was left to Zerubbabel to undertake the task of temple restoration. The work began in 520 B.C. with the blessing of the Persian ruler, Darius I. It continued until 515 B.C., when the job was finished and a great day of celebration was observed: "And the people of Israel, the priests and the Levites, and the rest of the returned exiles, celebrated the dedication of this house of God with joy [Ezra 6:16]."

Some seventy years later a servant in the palace of King Artaxerxes in the city of Susa had a different reason for wanting to make the long journey to Jerusalem. His name was Nehemiah. Word had come to him of the suffering of his fellow Jews in the homeland. Jerusalem, shorn of its protective walls, could offer to the resident Jews no protection against raiding bands from surrounding territories. Nehemiah received permission from the king to go to Jerusalem in order to take measures to alleviate the sufferings of his people. He not only received permission but was allotted supplies for the rebuilding of the walls and gates of Jerusalem. Nehemiah must have arrived in Jerusalem about the year 445 B.C. Shortly after he arrived, he made a secret inspection of the walls of the city by night, so that none of the Jews' enemies would know what he had in mind. Already two men named Sanballat and Tobiah were greatly displeased that Nehemiah had come with the king's blessing to aid the Jews. They were very suspicious of Nehemiah and were watching him closely.

NEHEMIAH: THE WALLS AND THE LAW

Nehemiah finally disclosed his plans to the leading men in Jerusalem and inspired them to begin immediately the task of building up the walls and gates of the city. With no hesitation, they gave themselves to the job before them. They were constantly under the watchful eyes of their enemies, who were waiting for a chance to attack the workers and put an end to their plans. To counteract this, Nehemiah devised a plan whereby half the people worked on the walls and gates while the other half held "the spears, shields, bows, and coats of mail." Some of the workers even labored with one hand and held their weapons with the other. At long last, however, the walls and the gates were finished. As in the case of the temple, a great day of celebration was observed and the wall dedicated. Such was the noise of the celebration that "the joy of Jerusalem was heard afar off."

Nehemiah also made certain reforms among the people. He saw to it that the Levites, who were the temple servants, received a living by being given their portion of the tithes. He also insisted on keeping the sabbath as a day holy to the Lord, rebuking those who tried to make it a day for selling and buying. What concerned him most, however, was the intermarriage between the Jews and those of other nations and cultures. He saw this to be a source of real corruption for his people. His concern is made evident by what he himself reports: "In those days also I saw the Jews who had married women of Ashdod, Ammon, and Moab; and half of their children spoke the language of Ashdod, and they could not speak the language of Judah, but the language of each people [Neh. 13:23–24]." So Nehemiah laid down the law: "I made them take oath in the name of God, saying, 'You shall not give your daughters to their sons, or take their daughters for your sons or for yourselves [Neh. 13:25].'"

The decree against the marriage of Jews with foreigners was meant as a protective measure. Only by keeping the nation pure, reasoned Nehemiah, could the Jews keep their religion pure. This idea was to be

106

pressed even farther by the scribe who followed Nehemiah to Jerusalem. That scribe was Ezra.

EZRA: DISSOLVING OF FOREIGN MARRIAGES

Unlike his two predecessors, he was not involved in a building campaign. His main purpose was to establish the Law as the basis for the life of the community. This Law was probably based on, or at least was similar to, the Deuteronomic Code. Thus on a particular day, a great congregation was gathered together at Jerusalem to hear the reading of the Law of Moses by Ezra the scribe. He stood on a wooden platform with the chief priests of the people on each side of him. At the proper time, he unrolled a scroll; out of respect, all the people stood up. As the Law was read and explained, the people listened intently. They felt that these were more than mere words of wisdom from an intelligent scribe. It was their conviction, as it was Ezra's conviction, that they represented a message from God. Such words must be obeyed. And apparently they were obeyed as the Law of the Jewish community.

Shortly after Ezra had given the people the Law, certain Israelite officials approached him and informed him of a situation that seriously distressed him. They told him how the exiles had married women of other lands and cultures. Wives had been taken from the Canaanites, the Hittites, the Perizzites, the Jebusites, the Ammonites, the Moabites, the Egyptians, and the Amorites. Foremost in doing this were certain officials and leaders of the community. In their words, "the holy race has mixed itself with the peoples of the lands." When Ezra heard this report, he reacted in the traditional manner of a mourner: "When I heard this, I rent my garments and my mantle, and pulled hair from my head and beard, and sat appalled [Ezra 9:3]."

He then lifted up his soul in prayer to God. In his prayer, he recalled the guilt of the Israelites and reviewed how God had given them into the hands of foreign rulers because of their guilt. But then God had shown favor toward Israel by permitting a remnant to return and to establish a "secure hold within his holy place." This latter inheritance was being endangered, said Ezra, by the people's breaking of God's commandments by intermarrying with peoples who were known for all kinds of unclean and abominable practices. After having prayed his prayer in the hearing of a crowd of people that had gathered about, Ezra concluded by saying:

> Wouldst thou not be angry with us till thou wouldst consume us, so that there should be no remnant, nor any to escape? O Lord the God of Israel, thou art just, for we are left a remnant that has escaped, as at this day. Behold, we are before thee in our guilt, for none can stand before thee because of this.
>
> —Ezra 9:14-15

The people in Ezra's hearing were cut to the quick. They felt themselves to be under the heavy burden of the guilt that Ezra had just pronounced, and they wept bitterly. One of their number, a man by the name of Shecaniah, became the spokesman for the group. He too shared the general feeling of guilt. He proposed a harsh remedy in the hope that God would yet be merciful: "We have broken faith with our God and have married foreign women from the peoples of the land, but even now there is hope for Israel in spite of this. Therefore let us make a covenant with our God to put away all these wives and their children [Ezra 10:2–3]."

Nehemiah had forbidden the marrying of foreign women because he was interested in keeping the "chosen people" a pure nation. Ezra went one step farther; he ordered dissolved every existing marriage between a Jew and a foreigner. The last chapter of Ezra's book contains a listing of the names of those who had to give up their wives and children because the latter were not of Jewish blood. There is little wonder that at the conclusion of this painful separation, when a special service of worship was held, "the people of Israel were assembled with fasting and in sackcloth." In preventing such intermarriage, both Nehemiah and Ezra felt that they were keeping Israel's religion pure. They believed that this was the will of the Lord for Israel.

ESTHER

But was this the way that Israel was meant to fulfill the destiny that God had for it? Ezra and Nehemiah would have answered yes. The writer of the book of Esther would also have said yes. For he too links God's purpose with Israel as a special people. He writes about a beautiful young Israelite woman whose courage and faith in God became the salvation of her people. Indeed, the book of Esther indicates a time when there was intense bitterness against the gentiles. And there are many today who would say that it was inevitable that the Jewish community should work out God's purposes for its members in the way that it did. Some say that circumstances forced the Jews to become exclusive, concerned with religious ceremony and the strict observance of the Law. It should be noted that the keeping of the Law was not necessarily the heavy burden that we imagine it to have been. If the Law were only a burden to the pious Jew, we would scarcely have such a psalm as this:

> The law of the Lord is perfect,
> reviving the soul;
> the testimony of the Lord is sure,
> making wise the simple;
> the precepts of the Lord are right,
> rejoicing the heart;

the commandment of the Lord is pure,
enlightening the eyes;
the fear of the Lord is clean,
enduring for ever;
the ordinances of the Lord are true,
and righteous altogether.
More to be desired are they than gold,
even much fine gold;
sweeter also than honey
and drippings of the honeycomb.
—Psalm 19:7–10

THE MACCABEES

From the time of Ezra to the advent of Jesus Christ, the Israelite community of faith struggled through 350 years of turbulent history. During most of this time Israel was a vassal of much greater powers. Some of its overlords included the Persians, the Greeks under Alexander the Great, the Ptolemies of Egypt, the Seleucids of Asia Minor, Syria, and finally the Romans. From 166 B.C. to 63 B.C., the Jews enjoyed at least a nominal amount of freedom under a group of leaders known as the Maccabees, named after Judas Maccabeus (the Hammerer). The Jews had refused to submit to the religious indignities imposed upon them by their rulers, especially those imposed by Antiochus IV. He had committed the "abomination of desolation" by sacrificing a pig on the altar of the temple in Jerusalem. This was the most blatant of many corruptions of the faith that they saw all about them. They revolted and were successful in restoring the purity and practice of temple worship as well as securing for themselves about a hundred years of freedom.

DANIEL

A book written during the Maccabean age that did much to encourage and inspire the adherents of Judaism was the book of Daniel. This is the story of how a man named Daniel and his friends endured all kinds of hardships in a foreign land and yet came out unscathed. It was just what the Jews of that time needed to give their morale a boost. Yet in this book, too, we see Israel's great concern for its own life as a nation and as a people. At the same time we see a genuine concern for the Law also.

During the entire postexilic period, or the period following 538 B.C., Israel's main concern seems to have turned inward on itself. Israel continually fought to keep itself from being corrupted by outside influences and to keep its religion pure and undefiled. Israel centered its concerns in the cult of temple worship and in the keeping of the Law. And in all this it believed that it was doing the will of God.

109

JONAH

But there were other voices in Israel that did not see Israel's destiny in terms of exclusiveness. They saw it in terms of inclusiveness. The writer of the imaginative little narrative known as the book of Jonah spoke of God's concern for Nineveh and portrayed God sending a prophet to preach repentance to that city. But Jonah, the unwilling prophet who reflected in himself the conservative and exclusive spirit of most Jews of his day, would have none of it and tried to run away. However, God persisted with Jonah, finally sending a great fish to swallow him and carry him back to his original destination. So Jonah went to Nineveh, preached repentance, and saw the people turn to God. This unexpected turn of events sorely distressed Jonah. He went outside the city and sat down in a booth that he made. Then God sent a plant to grow up over Jonah to provide even more shade. This pleased Jonah. But then a worm attacked the plant and it withered. The next day Jonah had to do without the shade afforded by the plant. This made him angrier than ever. At this point, God spoke to the prophet in words that the author meant for all the Jewish people:

> You pity the plant, for which you did not labor, nor did you make it grow, which came into being in a night, and perished in a night. And should not I pity Nineveh, that great city, in which there are more than a hundred and twenty thousand persons who do not know their right hand from their left, and also much cattle?
>
> —Jonah 4:10–11

The story of Jonah should not be taken as strict historical fact. Whales do not swallow people alive and spit them up still alive a few days later. We are meant to understand by this story that God has a concern for all nations, not for one privileged nation only. However, this was a message that postexilic Judaism did not seem to grasp.

RUTH

The writer of the story of Ruth had a somewhat similar motive. In contrast to the strict taboo on foreign marriages, he portrayed a marriage far back in Israelite history between a Moabite woman by the name of Ruth to a kindly Jew named Boaz. From this marriage was born a son named Obed, the father of Jesse, who was in turn the father of the great King David. Here was another voice protesting Israel's self-chosen way of fulfilling its destiny. But that voice was almost alone in Judaism.

A LIGHT TO THE NATIONS

As noted earlier, a prophet bearing the message of God's universal love was Second Isaiah. He had seen Israel as a servant who had suffered for

110

the welfare of the other nations of the earth. Through it, they would find their redemption. God had made Israel a light to the gentiles. Because of Israel's mission, all the ends of the earth would see the salvation of God. Second Isaiah saw Israel's destiny as that of a servant who would bring in a new age for all humankind.

As Christians look at the history of Israel, they cannot help but feel that Israel did not fulfill this vision of its mission. Israel's concern for its own national life and cultural identity seemed to blind it to the servant role envisioned by Second Isaiah. Whatever the reason, it does not seem that Israel accepted the role of "a light to the nations" or a "covenant to the people." In this sense, we should have to say that Israel did not fulfill the destiny that we believe God had for it. And yet if that destiny and that purpose were not fulfilled by Israel as a nation, it was to find its fulfillment in one who was an Israelite and of the lineage of David. If the remnant of Israel did not accept the servant role to humankind, there was yet to be another who would take the form of a servant, that through him all persons might be blessed and become sons and daughters of the covenant. With that remnant of One, a whole new act in the biblical drama begins. It is an act so radically different that it is like moving from the old to the new. Indeed, that is exactly what it is.

Part Two

THE NEW COVENANT

PALESTINE IN JESUS' DAY

THE NEW COVENANT IN JESUS CHRIST

Getting a Perspective

When you began to read this book, you did not begin with the story of creation in the first chapter of Genesis. You read an introductory chapter first, in which I explained that the history of Israel as a nation really began with the event of the exodus under the leadership of Moses shortly after 1300 B.C. This event was seen by the Israelites as a great act of deliverance at the hand of God. As their historians looked back into the past, they looked at all that happened prior to the exodus as God's preparation of their people for a great role in history. So when we read the stories of the patriarchs, or even the stories of the beginnings of things, we know that they were written or edited by persons who had a strong faith in God, a God who had chosen Israel as a special people. What they wrote, they wrote from the perspective of their faith. When we are able to understand that, we are ready to proceed with the story that the Bible tells, beginning with the creation.

What is necessary for the understanding of the Old Testament account is also necessary before we take up the life of Jesus. There are certain things that must first be said, so that we may understand the meaning of the story of Jesus.

Where, then, do we begin? The following personal incident may help to introduce the New Covenant portion of our story.

At a state park, a campfire burned brightly in the night. Its light helped to make visible some fishermen and a canoeist as they slowly and silently drifted by on the river below a small bluff. Across the river, shadows danced on the side of the cliff that rose one hundred feet straight up from the water. The night was cool, and the heat given off by the fire was just as welcome as its light. While logs crackled and flames leaped, the campfire gave its campers a good feeling. After a while, however, it went out. Its logs were then nothing but ashes; its flames no longer leaped in forked fury. It gave off very little heat then, and almost no light. The river was a dark void where only an occasional splash could be heard. The sheer face of the cliff beyond was no longer discernible.

115

Some two thousand years ago there was a little group of disciples who also felt a radiance and a warmth. They felt it in companionship with Jesus of Galilee. Never had they known such a one before. His presence, his words, his actions were as a great light that kindled living fires in their own lives. It gave them a good feeling to be with him. He caused a great hope to surge up within them when they thought of what he and they might accomplish together. They believed that he was the leader that their nation needed. In the glow of his presence, their aspirations were unbounded and their hearts were glad.

But then the flame that had burned so brightly among them was snuffed out. The light was no more. No longer were they to walk the dusty roads of Palestine together. Never again were they to hear words of truth from his lips, words that sounded like the ringing of a bell. And what of their hopes, their aspirations? As far as they were concerned, these had been cruelly dashed to the ground. Their despair is reflected in one of the postresurrection stories that are found in the Gospel of Luke. Two disciples were journeying from Jerusalem, the scene of Jesus' death on the cross, to the little town of Emmaus. It had been three days since the terrible deed, and their hearts were heavy as they walked. Then a stranger joined them and asked them why they were so sad. They told him what had just happened in the capital city. Among other things, they said: "But we had hoped that he was the one to redeem Israel [Luke 24:21]."

Notice the past perfect tense in those words. Jesus had been cruelly put to death on trumped-up charges. Now all the grand ideas they had had and all the words and promises of Jesus meant nothing. The last spark of hope had burned out. In the crucified figure on the hill of Golgotha, their world had come to an end. But had it? The Gospel writers had something more to say.

At the very moment when the disciples were overwhelmed with grief and despair, there came a cry through the darkness of the gloom that surrounded them: *He is risen! He is risen! Jesus lives!*

It was true. He was present with them. They remembered how he had told them that he would be crucified and that in three days he would rise again. The women who had been so dedicated to him, the rambunctious Peter, the beloved John, the skeptical Thomas, and all the disciples knew that Jesus was alive. He was real to them now, just as he had always been. They were not yet sure what lay ahead. How they were to serve this master had not been made plain to them. They knew in time it would be. But now, right now, it was enough to know that their master was with them. Their joy knew no bounds. They needed only to wait for further directions. This they did in a spirit of prayer and expectancy. The second chapter of the book of Acts records what happened to this little group of

Christians when, fifty days after Jesus' resurrection, they were together in the attitude of prayer.

PENTECOST

The place was an upstairs room in a modest house in the city of Jerusalem. It was the time of the Jewish festival of Pentecost when devout Jews brought offerings to the temple of the firstfruits of the harvest. That would have been the end of May or the beginning of June, according to our calendar. It was an important festival; it drew to Jerusalem both Jews and gentiles from all parts of the civilized world. In the midst of all the celebration, a few devout persons were together in prayerful and silent expectation. What happened is described in Acts:

> When the day of Pentecost had come, they were all together in one place. And suddenly a sound came from heaven like the rush of a mighty wind, and it filled all the house where they were sitting. And there appeared to them tongues as of fire, distributed and resting on each one of them. And they were all filled with the Holy Spirit and began to speak in other tongues, as the Spirit gave them utterance.
> —Acts 2:1-4

"Wind" and "tongues as of fire" are meant to convey to the reader the tremendous surging in and upon the disciples of the *power* of the Holy Spirit. At Pentecost, the author is trying to tell us, the disciples were visited with the power and the might of the Holy Spirit. It was this power that thrust them forth to witness. It is their witness that tells us more than anything else that the Holy Spirit had truly caught hold of them.

Filled up and running over with this experience, the disciples burst into the congested business district of the city. Their utterance was so ecstatic that some in the crowd shouted, "They're drunk!" Others stood perplexed and marveled.

THE WITNESS OF PETER

A spokesman for the little group stepped forward. It was Peter. He spoke straight and clear. The words that he uttered rang in many ears. These words are most important to us, for they represent what was perhaps the earliest recorded witness to the Christian faith. Peter's words were those of one who had known the Jesus of the flesh and who now worshiped him as Lord and Christ. His witness, in part, was:

> Men of Israel, hear these words: Jesus of Nazareth, a man attested to you by God with mighty works and wonders and signs which God did through him in your midst, as you yourselves know—this Jesus,

delivered up according to the definite plan and foreknowledge of God, you crucified and killed by the hands of lawless men. But God raised him up, having loosed the pangs of death, because it was not possible for him to be held by it. . . . Let all the house of Israel therefore know assuredly that God has made him both Lord and Christ, this Jesus whom you crucified.

—Acts 2:22-24, 36

In such words, Peter spoke. It was a witness that was given by the power of the Holy Spirit within him. It was given by one who knew beyond all doubt that Jesus, the carpenter of Nazareth, the prophet of Galilee, the teacher of authority, the healer of the sick, the proclaimer of the kingdom of God's love, and the voluntary sufferer on the cross—that this one had risen from the dead and was Messiah and Lord.

THE PRISM OF CRUCIFIXION AND RESURRECTION

What convinced Peter that Jesus was his Lord and Savior? The events in the life of Jesus that are of key importance in the speech made by Peter are: "you crucified and killed" and "but God raised him up." The two events that stand out here, and that stand out in all the early preaching of the apostles, are the crucifixion and resurrection of Jesus Christ. To these they constantly pointed as the climax of God's working in and through Jesus. Jesus became Lord to Peter and to the other disciples not in spite of but because of his death on a cross. In that man on a cross, they saw one who was willing to die to fulfill God's purpose for the people. In this, Jesus showed his followers how deep his love was for them. In this, they came to see how deep was the love of God for them. But, of course, it was not alone Jesus' death on a cross that made him Lord for Peter and the others. If it had all stopped on Golgotha, there would be no good news to preach. What made Jesus Lord and Christ was that his crucifixion was followed by his resurrection. The power of God's love was not to be defeated; the purpose that God had set about to accomplish through Jesus was not to be denied. By a mighty act, which must always remain a mystery, Jesus was raised from the dead and his spirit spread abroad in the world.

The mode of his resurrection, or just how it happened, is not the most important thing. It is enough to say here that this is a constant refrain of the early witness to Jesus by his first followers: "And with great power the apostles gave their testimony to the resurrection of the Lord Jesus, and great grace was upon them all [Acts 4:33]."

Central then to the preaching of the early apostles was the crucifixion and resurrection of Jesus Christ. Their outlook on the whole life of Jesus was colored by this twofold event. The crucifixion and resurrection of Jesus became a prism through which his first followers viewed his life. In this twofold event, the central meaning of his ministry was summed up.

118

And in this twofold event comes the climax of the whole biblical drama of salvation—the New Covenant in Jesus Christ.

EXODUS AND CRUCIFIXION/RESURRECTION

As the exodus is the pivot around which the Old Testament revolves, so the crucifixion-resurrection is the pivot around which the New Testament turns. As Christians, we believe the whole drama of salvation in both Old Testament and New Testament is most clearly seen through the prism of Jesus' death and resurrection. In other words, we see the whole Old Testament story as leading up to the life, death, and resurrection of Jesus. And we see the story of the Christian church, beginning at Pentecost, stemming from it. It is the highest point of our faith, toward which all paths lead in and from which all paths lead out.

Just as the exodus meant delivery from bondage, so Christians believe that the crucifixion-resurrection event means delivery from slavery. However, there is a great difference. The exodus meant freedom for a particular people, the Israelites. The crucifixion-resurrection event means a freedom for all humankind. The exodus meant deliverance from political slavery. The crucifixion-resurrection event means deliverance from spiritual slavery with all the implications that has for both individuals and society. In the exodus, God sent Moses to be the spokesman. In the crucifixion-resurrection event, God, through the person of Jesus, becomes our Deliverer. "And the Word became flesh and dwelt among us [John 1:14]."

GOD'S UNIVERSAL CONCERN

In the Old Testament story, the people tried to keep their covenant with God by obeying the Law—something that they were never fully able to do. In the New Testament story, God approaches us in the full sunburst of Divine Love and helps us to do the only thing that is necessary—to trust in God as a child would trust a loving parent. The Old Covenant story comes to an end with Israel's failure to be a "light for the Gentiles." The New Covenant story, as reported in the Gospel of Luke, begins with the declaration that God's universal purpose for humankind is about to be fulfilled:

> Lord, now lettest thou thy servant depart in peace,
> according to thy word;
> for mine eyes have seen thy salvation
> which thou hast prepared in the presence of all peoples,
> a light for revelation to the Gentiles,
> and for glory to thy people Israel.
>
> —Luke 2:29–32

This same universal note of the New Covenant is struck at the ending of the crucifixion-resurrection event as reported in the Gospel of Matthew:

> Now the eleven disciples went to Galilee, to the mountain to which Jesus had directed them. And when they saw him they worshiped him; but some doubted. And Jesus came and said to them, "All authority in heaven and on earth has been given to me. Go therefore and make disciples of all nations, baptizing them in the name of the Father and of the Son and of the Holy Spirit, teaching them to observe all that I have commanded you; and lo, I am with you always, to the close of the age."
>
> —Matthew 28:16–20

THE ONE COVENANT

We have followed the winding of the cord of the covenant through the Old Testament. We shall continue to follow it through the life of Jesus and the beginnings of the church in the New Testament. As we do so, we shall come to see that there is really only one covenant, whether it be in the Old or the New Testament—the covenant whereby God pours out blessing upon blessing on the people and expects only their trust in return. What, then, is new about it? Just this. In the New Testament Jesus of Nazareth, in whom is the fullness of God, comes to us, takes us by the hand, and introduces us personally to our Creator. Jesus makes it so much easier for us to trust in God because in him we see what God is really like.

THE CENTRALITY OF THE CRUCIFIXION/ RESURRECTION

A cross has stood for two thousand years as the symbol of the great love that God has for all people. An empty tomb has stood as the symbol of the new life that comes to those who trust in God with heart, mind, soul and body. Certainly the early followers of Jesus believed this. As they gave their witness to him, his crucifixion and resurrection were most on their lips. Certainly the writers of the four Gospels—Matthew, Mark, Luke and John—felt this way. The account of the last week of Jesus' life, leading up to and including his crucifixion and resurrection, comprises about one fourth of each of the Gospels.

If these writers chose to devote so much space to one small portion of Jesus' entire life, it must have been because it was especially important to them. Could it be that it was Jesus' death and resurrection that more than anything else made him Lord for them? All the evidence would seem to point to an affirmative answer.

If this is so, it is something to bear in mind as we read the various accounts of Jesus' life in the Gospels. We must always remember that the Gospel writers wrote about one who had already become, for them, both

120

Lord and Savior. They were not writing as objective historians, presenting the cold facts of Jesus' life. They were telling through everything they wrote what Jesus meant to them. They were writing, quite simply, in order that Jesus might become Lord and Savior for others who did not know him.

Of course, each Gospel writer had his own particular reason for writing an account of Jesus' life, and I shall examine those reasons briefly. But they were all one in wanting to bring their Lord to others. The fact that the Gospel writers loved Jesus colored what they set down about him. And it should have! Whether they were talking about his birth, his teachings, or his healing miracles, they were talking about one who was already their Lord.

Why should not five thousand be fed with a couple of fish and five loaves of bread? Why should not the dead be raised? What is to prevent a paralytic from being healed? This was Jesus, Lord and Christ, who walked the roads of Palestine. This was Jesus, with God's own Spirit within him, who moved among the people. What miracles were not possible when the Son of God dwelt with them!

So those who were the writers of the Gospels delved into their own store of knowledge and into the fund of knowledge about Jesus that already existed within the early Christian community and set down the four accounts of Jesus' life as we have them at the beginning of our New Testament. While presenting the same underlying testimony to Jesus, each Gospel nevertheless gives its own unique picture of him.

MARK

The Gospel of Mark was written about A.D. 70. This makes it the earliest of the Gospels. We are not certain who the author was, although tradition has assigned its authorship to one called John Mark, a young associate of the early apostles and Paul. But if he did not write it, why does it bear his name? The practice in those days of appending the name of a well-known personality to a writing, thereby helping to ensure its popularity and acceptance, suggests one answer to this question. This may or may not have been the case with Mark's Gospel. It does not really matter. The important thing is that we have it.

The Gospel of Mark was probably written in Rome for Roman Christians who found themselves in a difficult situation. Untold numbers of Christians had just lost their lives under the terrible persecutions inspired by Nero, the mad Roman emperor. The need of the hour was for a word of courage, comfort, and inspiration. By portraying Jesus as the divine Son of God who moved with courage through the various trials and tribulations that met him, the author was helping these early Christians to take heart. With that purpose in mind, he confined himself almost exclusively to

121

those incidents and those teachings of Jesus that would be a source of strength to people who might face death at any moment. This may be one of the reasons why Mark's Gospel is so short.

Drawing on the knowledge about Jesus that existed in the early Christian community at Rome, the author set down those remembrances he felt most valid for the time. These included many of Jesus' mighty acts, some of his teachings, a general outline of his ministry which became the basic pattern for the later Gospels, and an extensive account of the last week of his life, highlighted by his death and resurrection.

MATTHEW

The Gospel of Matthew was written about the year A.D. 100. Again we cannot say with certainty that its author is the one whose name it bears. Matthew, the disciple, may have had something to do with gathering many of Jesus' sayings that were later used in the book. However, the book itself comes from an unknown hand. Someone writing in eastern Syria, north of Palestine, used the Gospel of Mark as a base. He also used another source of material, the name of which we do not know, so we give it the symbol Q. This is from the German word *Quelle*, meaning source. This Q material was a collection of "sayings" or "teachings" of Jesus, which has since been lost. "Sayings" or "teachings" from the Q source are those that are not found in Mark's Gospel but that are found in both Matthew and Luke. If you want to look at some of these, compare Matthew 5:1–3, 6, 11–12 with Luke 6:20–23; or Matthew 5:46–48 with Luke 6:32–33, 36; or Matthew 7:1–5 with Luke 6:37–38, 41–42. In addition, the author of the Gospel of Matthew included material found only in his record. This we designate as M. Except for the genealogical list found at the beginning of the book, this material peculiar to his Gospel probably came out of the oral tradition (stories or teachings of Jesus circulated by word of mouth). A good example of M is found in the first and second chapters of Matthew.

Why was Matthew written? About the turn of the first century A.D., Christians were in need of a standard for their faith. They wanted answers to many important questions. Was Jesus really human? Is the Old Testament of any value? Does the authority of the church really go back to the twelve apostles? The Gospel of Matthew helped to provide that standard. It became a manual for instruction, with an accent on the teachings of Jesus. The genealogy at the beginning served to emphasize Jesus' human roots in Hebrew history as well as to prove that Jesus was the long-awaited Messiah. The inclusion of many references to the Old Testament was the author's way of indicating the importance of the Hebrew scriptures.

LUKE

When we come to the Gospel of Luke we have a different problem. We cannot speak of that Gospel by itself, but we must consider it along with the Acts of the Apostles. Luke and Acts were written as one complete work in two volumes by the same author. The Gospel of Luke traces the life of Jesus from birth through his death and resurrection. The Acts of the Apostles takes up where Luke leaves off, and traces the spread of the early Christian church. Because the style of writing in both books is so similar, those scholars who study such matters very carefully have long felt that they must have been written by the same person. Was Luke the physician and companion of Paul, to whom the latter refers in Colossians 4:14? There has been a great deal of debate about this, but the general opinion is that Luke is the author of both the Gospel and the Acts.

The Gospel of Luke was most likely written between A.D. 80 and 85. The writing of the Acts probably followed immediately afterward. What was Luke's purpose in writing? His own preface to the Gospel tells us:

> Inasmuch as many have undertaken to compile a narrative of the things which have been accomplished among us, just as they were delivered to us by those who from the beginning were eyewitnesses and ministers of the word, it seemed good to me also, having followed all things closely for some time past, to write an orderly account for you, most excellent Theophilus, that you may know the truth concerning the things of which you have been informed.
>
> —Luke 1:1–4

Luke's purpose was to present a history of the Christian faith from the birth of Jesus through the time of Paul ("to write an orderly account"), and thus to convince others of the greatness and uniqueness of the Christian faith ("that you may know the truth"). Aside from his stated purpose, the nature of his book reveals many other concerns and interests. His was a conscious attempt throughout to show that this new faith was not trying to undermine the power of Rome. This met a real need, since Christians had previously been made the scapegoats of Roman persecution. Witness how the author portrays in Luke 20:20–26 Jesus' attitude toward the state. The author desired also to show that Christianity was a world faith, a faith for all nations. Luke puts a great deal of emphasis on the work of the Holy Spirit, the place of prayer in the life of Jesus, and the role of women. And his treatment of the birth of Jesus is even fuller than that of Matthew. One cannot read the Gospel of Luke without sensing a note of joy that runs from beginning (Luke 2:14) to end (Luke 24:53).

The Gospel of Luke, as well as the Acts of the Apostles, was most probably written in the city of Rome for gentile Christians, to be used in their worship and teaching. Like Matthew, Luke used the basic outline and material of Mark. He also used material from the Q source. Finally he included a great many things that are not found in the other Gospels. To this material we give the symbol L. This includes among other things the birth and infancy stories, accounts of the passion and resurrection peculiar to him, and parables such as the good Samaritan and the prodigal son.

JOHN

The writing of the Gospel of John seems best dated shortly after A.D. 100. We do not know the name of the author, but it is clear that when the Gospel first appeared, the hope was that the apostle John would be accepted as its author. From the writings of the author, even though we do not know his name, we can infer some things about him. He was probably a leader in the Christian church of his day. He may have written also First, Second, and Third John. He was thoroughly familiar with the life of Jesus and with Jewish customs and geography. He most likely wrote this Gospel in the city of Ephesus, one of the early Christian centers of the Mediterranean world.

The author makes clear to us why he wrote: "Now Jesus did many other signs in the presence of the disciples, which are not written in this book; but these are written that you may believe that Jesus is the Christ, the Son of God, and that believing you may have life in his name [John 20:30–31]."

Thus Jesus is presented to the reader of this Gospel as the Son of God, through whom the will of God was made known. Jesus is called the eternal Logos or "Word" of God in the first chapter. By this the author meant that Jesus was with God from the beginning, and that he was the perfect "wisdom" of God. This idea emphasizes the divine nature of Jesus.

Nevertheless, the Gospel of John is very quick to present the human nature of Jesus. This Gospel speaks of Jesus as one who became angry, who thirsted, who grieved, who suffered, and who died. It was very important, incidentally, for the Gospel to be clear about the fact that Jesus was thoroughly human. There was a brand of religious thinking current at the end of the first century A.D. by the name of Docetism. One of the peculiar ideas of Docetism was that Jesus Christ, being the Son of God, could not possibly have defiled himself by putting on human flesh. It only seemed as if he did, but actually he never really was human; so he could not have suffered and died. It was all an illusion. Such thought had no basis in fact, but many people were led to believe it. The author of the Gospel was well aware of the Docetic doctrines. He therefore sought to refute them in the very first chapter of his book: "And the Word became flesh and dwelt among us, full of grace and truth [John 1:14]."

The power, presence, and promise of the Holy Spirit; the rebirth needed by humankind, and the eternal life that is possible for people here and now are other positive themes dealt with in this Gospel. It has long been felt that the Synoptic Gospels (Matthew, Mark, and Luke) give us a more historically accurate account of Jesus' life than does the Gospel of John. The latter tends to be more theological; that is, it tends to be less concerned with the actual reporting of the event and more concerned to develop the meanings behind the event. For example, the account of the feeding of the five thousand in John 6 is followed by a long discourse about

Jesus as "the bread of life." Yet there are places where the Gospel of John may be more correct than the other three. This would indicate that while the author of John was most likely acquainted with the Synoptic Gospels, or traditions behind them, he also drew on some independent sources of his own.

With this background, we are ready to begin in chronological order the story of the life of Jesus.

Scene 1.
GOD WAS IN CHRIST

ROME, PALESTINE, AND JEWISH EXPECTATIONS

Who could possibly have guessed what was happening on that night in the year 6 B.C.? Certainly not the emperor of the mighty Roman Empire or any of his advisers or generals—not even Herod the Great, who ruled over Judea. Of course, Rome tried to make it a point to know everything that was going on in the empire. If there was discontentment or a sign of revolt anywhere, immediately the famous Roman legions would be dispatched to the spot to squelch any outbreak of violence. The Roman legions were so powerful that none dared to challenge their might. If they did, defeat and disaster were assured. The Roman rulers were particularly interested at this time in the events happening in Palestine.

Perhaps this seems odd. On a map of the Mediterranean world over which Rome ruled, Palestine appears as only a tiny spot. It does not seem that this small country could have been of great importance to Rome. But it was. For one thing, Palestine was a bridge between Asia Minor and Europe to the north and Egypt and Africa to the south. Trade routes passed through it to the east also. It was like the hub of a wheel. Then too, there were nations hostile to Rome not far from Palestine. Chief among these enemies of Rome were the Parthians. It was necessary, therefore, for Rome to maintain strong defenses in Palestine. It kept a close watch on Palestine because it felt that it was necessary to be aware of any undercurrents of unrest that might be occurring there.

Yet how could Rome possibly know that on a peaceful night in a small town in Palestine a life was coming into the world that would shake the very foundations of the Roman Empire. Who could have guessed what momentous event was taking place in, as tradition tells us, Bethlehem of Judea.

Certainly the people of Palestine or their leaders could not have guessed this. This is true even though they were looking for some kind of leader. But they did not expect their deliverer to be born to the poor

125

people of the land. They had been led to expect one who would come as a mighty conqueror on the clouds of heaven. With his heavenly armies, he would overthrow the oppressor (in this case, Rome) and make Jerusalem the capital of the nations.

All nations would come to Jerusalem, and then there would be peace for the world and prosperity and glory for Israel. All this would be made possible by one who would come to them as a "Son of man" from heaven. He would be a second David; indeed, he would be from David's royal lineage. This view of salvation is known by the term apocalypticism, and it came to be more and more the view held by the Jewish people just before the birth of Jesus. Needless to say, persons holding that idea of how the Messiah (God's anointed one) was to come, would hardly be looking for their Savior to be born of a poor family of Palestine.

And yet the Prince of Peace, the Son of God, was born into a carpenter's family. No royal trumpets heralded his arrival, no emissaries from Rome were present, no Jewish scribes recorded the event. Silently, silently the wondrous gift was given.

Jesus' Birth and the Crucifixion/Resurrection Perspective

Following Jesus' death and resurrection, it seemed incredible to Christians that he could have come into the world in such an ordinary way. He was their Lord and Savior. His life, suffering, death, and resurrection were no ordinary events. How then could anyone suppose that his birth had not been extraordinary? It was this kind of thinking that must have led inevitably to the circulation of certain stories and traditions that are now associated with the birth of Jesus. Nor would we give up a single one of them. The angelic announcement to Mary, the hymn of praise from her lips, the visit to Bethlehem, the birth in a stable, the song of the angels, the shepherds on a Galilean hillside and their visit to the manger, the journey and homage of the three wise men of the East—these stories have endeared themselves over the centuries to Christians. Much more than endearment, however, has come to us from these stories. They have told us, in their beautiful, poetic way, what cold, analytical facts could never tell us—that Jesus is the Son of God, that he is ruler of all nature and all the universe, that both the humble and the mighty must bow before him, and that in him as in no one else in all history, we have seen the very fullness of God.

It is important for us to remember here that Jesus became Lord for people by virtue of his resurrection. It was the resurrected Jesus that was preached by the first apostles. In the early speeches that we find in Acts, nothing is mentioned by Peter of the birth of Jesus. Paul, the first great missionary, makes no mention of Jesus' birth; evidently the details were not important to him. What mattered most to him, as we gather from his writings, was the crucified and risen Jesus. The Gospel of Mark and the Gospel of John both omit any mention of the birth of Jesus. And Matthew and Luke vary in the traditions that they have recorded about his birth.

What, then, does this say to us? It reminds us that we interpret the stories of the birth of Jesus from the same perspective that we interpret the other stories of his life; namely, that they were set down by persons for whom Jesus was already Lord and Master by virtue of his death on the cross and his resurrection from the dead. This was the double event that was of paramount importance to them, as the witness of the early Christians clearly shows. Luke, in his Gospel, could relate: "And the angel said to them, 'Be not afraid; for behold, I bring you good news of a great joy which will come to all the people; for to you is born this day in the city of David a Savior, who is Christ the Lord [Luke 2:10–11].'"

Why could Luke say this? Because for him Jesus was already Lord. The good news of a great joy had already been proclaimed and had become a fact when Jesus had risen from the dead. The birth stories tell us at the beginning of Jesus' life what the early disciples did not really know fully until the end of his life: Jesus is Lord and Savior, the Son of God. This helps us to understand better what both Matthew and Luke mean when they tell us that Jesus' birth was of the Holy Spirit. This is what is called the doctrine of the virgin birth. Such a concept holds that Jesus' birth did not come about as a result of sexual relations between a husband and wife.

Many people consider this doctrine very necessary for their faith. Yet we are faced with a disturbing question. If this doctrine was so important to Christian faith, why were Peter and Paul, and Mark's Gospel and John's Gospel, so quiet about it? Apparently it was not this that made Jesus Lord for them. Does this mean, then, that we do not honor the story of the virgin birth? Of course not!

Rather, we have to ask ourselves: What is this story really telling us? What does it really mean? The answer is not too hard to find. It serves to drive home that which is basic to the whole understanding of the life of Jesus: *God was in Christ.* The fullness of God's Spirit was in and upon Jesus from the moment of his birth and through all his life. Jesus was born fully human and fully divine. This view is called the doctrine of the incarnation. In his own deeply theological way, the author of the Gospel of John said the same thing:

> In the beginning was the Word, and the Word was with God, and the Word was God. He was in the beginning with God; all things were made through him, and without him was not anything made that was made. . . . And the Word became flesh and dwelt among us, full of grace and truth; we have beheld his glory, glory as of the only Son from the Father.
>
> —John 1:1–3, 14

JESUS' BIRTH AND EARLY LIFE

As nearly as we can tell, Jesus was born about 6 B.C. Now this may seem strange. If B.C. means "Before Christ," how could Jesus be born six years "Before Christ"? The explanation is that somewhere in the years between the birth of Jesus and our own day, someone made a mistake in the calendar. Somewhere along the line, six years were lost. In order to correct this error, the date of the birth of Jesus had to be moved back six years. That is why Jesus' birth is spoken of as 6 B.C.

His mother's name was Mary and his father's name was Joseph. He was part of a family that numbered at least four brothers and two sisters. Although tradition suggests that he was born in Bethlehem of Judea, he spent his life until the time of his active ministry in the town of Nazareth of Galilee. While his mother outlived him, it is supposed that his father died while Jesus was still at home. Jesus, therefore, probably became the breadwinner for the family. Since his father was a carpenter, Jesus very likely followed in that occupation.

Very little is known of Jesus' early life. Beyond the stories that deal with his birth and presentation in the temple (the latter found in Luke 2:22–38), we have only one incident from the boyhood of Jesus. This concerns a visit to the great temple of Jerusalem with his parents when he was twelve years old. Although it is only one single incident, it is very revealing in what it tells us.

According to Jewish custom, a boy was permitted to make a pilgrimage to the temple at Jerusalem when he reached his twelfth year. What an exciting event this must have been for Jesus! The trip probably took about three days. Jesus must have felt a special thrill when the gleaming walls and towers of the Holy City first came into view. The sight was enough to make even the most hardened pilgrim tingle with joy.

Jesus was captivated and enthralled in the bustling city of Jerusalem by one thing most of all—the great temple. That was the center of Jewish worship. There were to be found the scribes, who were the expert interpreters of the Jewish Law. In charge of the ceremonies of worship were the high priest and his assistants. Also connected with the temple was a lay society whose members were known as Pharisees—men who were most scrupulous about keeping every jot and tittle of the Law.

Evidently Jesus was given considerable freedom to roam about the city on his own. After the caravan heading for Nazareth had already started on its way, his mother and father realized belatedly that Jesus was not with their other relatives. So they hurried back to Jerusalem, wondering what could have happened to him. Finally they found him in the temple, sitting among the learned men and scholars of the time "listening to them and asking them questions." His parents were surprised at all this and a bit upset.

"Son," said his mother, "why have you treated us so? Behold, your father and I have been looking for you anxiously."

Jesus was in turn surprised, but for another reason: "How is it that you sought me?" he said. "Did you not know that I must be in my Father's house?"

Mary and Joseph did not quite understand Jesus' answer. But as devoted parents, they were overjoyed to have found their son. And although Jesus might have preferred to stay even longer in his "Father's house," the scripture reports: "And he went down with them and came to Nazareth, and was obedient to them; and his mother kept all these things in her heart [Luke 2:51]."

It is evident that the Gospel writer was attempting to show readers that Jesus, even in his youth, had a keen desire to learn more about God and God's will. He had already learned much from the stories that he heard from his mother and father in his own home. He learned even more in the synagogue school in Nazareth. His later parables also indicate that he must have had many thoughts about God as he trudged through open fields and up and down the hills surrounding his hometown. Perhaps it was only natural that a desire to learn took him to the temple, where for him time stood still.

A short story, yes. But a story that opens a window for us and lets us see the development of an ever closer and deeper relationship between God and Jesus—a relationship of love and trust. Here, even in Jesus' youth, the New Covenant was having its beginning and a new meaning for our lives was developing.

Scene 2.
A COMMITMENT AND A STRUGGLE

One day Jesus laid down his tools for the last time. Perhaps he stood back a pace and took stock of the door he had just finished for a customer at the other side of the village. Tomorrow he would deliver it, and then he was finished. No longer would he ply the trade of a carpenter. Another work was calling, a work for which he had been destined from the day of his birth. And now he must heed the summons.

His decision to quit the carpenter shop and to give himself to another kind of work was not made hastily. Many weeks, months, and years were spent in the making of it. And who is able to say what struggles of the soul he endured before the decision was finally made. This is something hidden from our eyes, something we shall never know. But he did resolve to journey from his home in Nazareth to Judea in the south. Then he traveled to that spot in the Jordan River where John the Baptist was doing his work calling people to repentance for their own sins and for the sins of their nation, baptizing them as the sign of God's forgiveness and of their desire to live a new life.

JOHN THE BAPTIST

At this place Jesus committed himself to the new work that he was to do. But why here? Why should he make this commitment in connection with the ministry of John and associate it with John's practice of baptism? Indeed, if Jesus was God's Son, why did he have to be baptized at all? It probably seemed perfectly natural for Jesus to begin his ministry and make his commitment in connection with the small movement that had already begun with John. The birth stories in Luke suggest that Jesus and John may have been cousins. How much they saw of each other, we do not know. Jesus must certainly have been aware of John's work, for it had stirred the whole countryside. Multitudes of people came to hear him, although not all for the same reason.

Some of those who came were not exactly sympathetic to what he had to say. The Pharisees (the zealous keepers of the Law) and the Sadducees (religious conservatives, most of whom came from the priestly aristocracy) would hardly be awestruck by his message, since one of his most scathing denunciations was directed against them. Oh, how they must have wanted to silence him! This is what he said to them:

> You brood of vipers! Who warned you to flee from the wrath to come? Bear fruit that befits repentance, and do not presume to say to yourselves, "We have Abraham as our father"; for I tell you, God is able from these stones to raise up children to Abraham. Even now the axe is laid to the root of the trees; every tree therefore that does not bear good fruit is cut down and thrown into the fire.
>
> —Matthew 3:7–10

There can be little question that John had risen as a figure commanding attention on the Palestinian scene. He was a crude-looking fellow. His dress consisted of a rough camel's hair garment that extended from the shoulders to the knees. Around his waist he wore a wide leather belt. Such dress, together with his unshaven features, must have given him a formidable appearance. Although he would be classed as an eccentric person by many, this did not diminish the urgency with which he proclaimed his message. Indeed, it added to it. For here people saw one whose concern was not with the pleasures of this life but with the salvation of his nation's people. And to that purpose he gave every ounce of his strength. It was to this man, then, that Jesus came.

JESUS' BAPTISM

But why did Jesus have to be baptized? This has been a thorny question for many. It was so for the first Christians. One of the Gospels deals with the question. According to Matthew's account, John raised the question when Jesus came to him to be baptized: "I need to be baptized by you, and do you come to me?" Jesus answered: "Let it be so now; for thus it is fitting for us to fulfil all righteousness."

How would Jesus "fulfil all righteousness"? He would do so by identifying himself with the sins of his people, his nation. Though the sins and mistakes of his nation were not his fault, as a citizen of the nation he felt himself involved in the guilt of his people. He did not stand aloof from them, pitying them from afar. Nor did he say to himself: "I, of course, am perfect, so I do not really need this baptism, but for the sake of you poor souls, I will submit to it, just to let you know that I am on your side."

This kind of thinking would be foreign to the whole spirit and life of Jesus. He felt himself to be part of the whole situation in which his people had separated themselves from God. His identification with them in this situation was painfully real. His baptism was the baptism of one who felt personally the burden of his people's waywardness. He was linked with them in their struggles, their aspirations, their fears, and their misgivings. He was also linked with those who came seeking baptism and a new life. As a Jew, he came to be baptized with other devout Jews. Thus he aligned himself at that moment in a dramatic way not only with the sin of his people but also with their hope for salvation.

So Jesus came feeling, as he must have, that this was the most natural point at which to begin his own ministry. In simple language Mark reports: "In those days Jesus came from Nazareth of Galilee and was baptized by John in the Jordan [Mark 1:9]."

But there is more. Here we come again to the attempt to describe in human symbols a spiritual experience. This is always difficult. Perhaps this is the way Jesus described his experience to his disciples at a later time. Perhaps it is the writer's way of trying to describe it. At any rate, the experience itself is attested to in each of the four Gospels. It must have been a very moving moment for Jesus: "And when he came up out of the water, immediately he saw the heavens opened and the Spirit descending upon him like a dove; and a voice came from heaven, 'Thou art my beloved Son; with thee I am well pleased [Mark 1:10-11].'"

JESUS' COMMITMENT

Jesus had the conviction of having been chosen by God to fulfill a special mission. This mission was not as yet clearly spelled out in all its details.

But that he had one, he had no doubt. God's hand was upon him, God's Spirit was in him, and God had blessed him. He knew that he whom God blesses is blessed for a purpose. This was a time of commitment for Jesus. In this moment he must certainly have had a high sense of destiny. He was no longer just one of many who had come to be baptized by John; he was not just one sharing in the act of repentance and forgiveness along with others. He was from that moment on committed to a task of telling these people, and all who would listen, just what it meant to turn to God.

Jesus' experience of baptism had deep meaning for the people of his own time and country, although right then they were not aware of it. Christians of every age, looking back on this event, have felt that it had very deep meaning for them too. And so we do today. For in Jesus Christ we see one who comes to us sharing our doubts, our fears, and our feelings of guilt and shame. And yet even as he comes and kneels beside us when we are truly sorry for the wrong we have done, so also he rises up with us, takes us by the hand, and leads us to our God. This is why he came; to this end he was born.

If the baptismal event was crucial in the life of Jesus, so also was his temptation experience in the Judean wilderness. As pictured for us in the Gospel accounts of Matthew and Luke, the temptation of Jesus included a personal devil, stones that could become bread, the pinnacle of the temple, a high mountain, and the kingdoms of the world. Yet we are to remember again that this is an attempt to picture a spiritual and inward experience by means of external symbols. There is no other way to express forcefully this wilderness wrestling of Jesus.

Jesus had already committed himself to a great task that lay before him. There was no question of this anymore. The decision had been made. He was to bring persons to God. But just how was he to go about it? How was he to approach people? What kind of leader was he to be? What should he tell them? These and other questions begged for answers. Clearly it was a time for honest soul-searching. A place of solitude was needed. This was a time for retreat, a brief pause before a titanic struggle was to begin.

JESUS' STRUGGLE

The place of retreat was most probably somewhere in the wilderness region between Jerusalem and the Dead Sea. Here were broad stretches of mountainous, barren terrain where one could easily be alone without fear of interference.

Some of the key ideas with which Jesus wrestled at this time were shared by him with his disciples at a later date. As we study each of these, we shall see how they were intimately bound up with the task that lay ahead of him. "And he fasted forty days and forty nights, and afterward he

132

was hungry. And the tempter came and said to him, 'If you are the Son of God, command these stones to become loaves of bread [Matt. 4:2-3].'"

This suggests the primary question that came to the mind of Jesus in this time of retreat: *What are the real needs of persons to which I should give myself?* Linked to this might well have come a second question: Are the deepest needs of persons necessarily those that are most obvious? Jesus knew, for example, what it meant to be poor. He grew up among the poor of the land. His own family was numbered among those who did not have great material possessions. It is not too much to imagine that he may have known what it meant to be hungry. Poverty was to be seen on every hand. Except for a few privileged individuals, most of the people barely eked out an existence. If they had any hope at all of having a little extra, the oppressive Roman taxes soon wiped that out. No wonder that the tax collectors were so hated by the people.

Knowing well the conditions of his own people and seeing the distress of the poor on every side, Jesus could not evade the problem of poverty. As one who had been called to lead, did he have a duty to try to improve the economic status of his people? Should he do all in his power to feed the hungry, clothe the naked, and shelter the homeless?

THE DEEPEST NEED

The physical needs of his people must have cried out to him. He must have been painfully tempted to direct *all* his energies and abilities toward the meeting of these needs. Yet Jesus realized that to minister solely to the physical needs of people would not really be meeting their deepest problem. It would be wrong for him to do anything other than to meet the deepest need they had. What was that need? "But he answered, 'It is written, "Man shall not live by bread alone, but by every word that proceeds from the mouth of God [Matt. 4:4]."'"

The people's deepest need was to live in a closer, more meaningful relationship with God. Because they did not, their relationships with one another were strained. Because their relationships with one another were strained, the rich had little concern for those who had nothing. So poverty, injustice, prejudice, and other ills of society were but the outward symptoms of a much more serious inward disease, a disease of the spirit. It was the disease of persons living apart from God, who were consequently living apart from one another.

Jesus saw that what they needed most was to know God with all their heart and mind and soul and strength. From this all good stemmed. During his ministry Jesus would feed the hungry, heal the sick, and help people in a variety of physical ways. But always as he served people he would be opening up for them a new relationship with God. In this way he

133

served their deepest need. Upon this primary decision to serve the people's deepest need, the other two decisions recorded in the temptation narrative are dependent. Let us look at them briefly.

> Then the devil took him to the holy city, and set him on the pinnacle of the temple, and said to him, "If you are the Son of God, throw yourself down; for it is written,
> 'He will give his angels charge of you,'
> and
> 'On their hands they will bear you up,
> lest you strike your foot against a stone.'"
> Jesus said to him, "Again it is written, 'You shall not tempt the Lord your God.'"
>
> —Matthew 4:5-7

This temptation had to do with how Jesus would conduct his ministry. He was being tempted to use various supernatural signs and feats of magic to capture the interest of the crowd. People are always wanting to see the unusual. To appeal to this human desire would surely produce a large following.

In spite of performing many wondrous healing acts—to which we must give the name of miracle because we do not understand them—Jesus chose to give himself to a patient, day-by-day ministry to people in order to reveal God's love for them and to help them to discover their need for that love. Jesus lived out his ministry in a way designed to show people how they were meant to live in God's world. As they saw how Jesus lived, they came to know how they were to live.

> Again, the devil took him to a very high mountain, and showed him all the kingdoms of the world and the glory of them; and he said to him, "All these I will give you, if you will fall down and worship me."
> Then Jesus said to him, "Begone, Satan! for it is written,
> 'You shall worship the Lord your God
> and him only shall you serve.'"
>
> —Matthew 4:8–10

Should Jesus lead his people in a revolt against the power of Rome and set up a new Jewish state? Should he fashion a kingdom after the other great kingdoms of the earth? Jesus' answer to these questions was no. He had not come for that purpose. He was not primarily interested in national boundaries or political power. He was concerned that people worship and serve God. The kingdom he was interested in was the kingdom of God. For this kingdom he would give his life.

Here at the beginning of his ministry, Jesus wrestled with the question of just what direction his life would take. It was quite a spiritual struggle. At the end of it he emerged with a clear conviction of what he was to do.

134

He was to heal the rift between God and God's people and bring them into the life of the kingdom. In so doing, he would become the herald of a New Covenant—a covenant of love, forgiveness, justice, joy, and peace. He set himself immediately to this task.

Scene 3.
A NEW KIND OF KINGDOM

Old people whose faces bore the marks of years nodded their heads in silent approval. Young people with most of life yet before them listened in open-eyed wonder. Mothers and fathers and their children pressed close. Twelve men, handpicked by Jesus, stood nearby in order not to lose a word. The carpenter from Nazareth was speaking to them. The words that he spoke met a longing in their souls that gave him their raptured attention. How simply he spoke, yet how full of wisdom. It was like a great banquet, being in his presence and feasting on the truth he offered. No one had ever spoken like that before. Something in him touched something in them, and they could not be quite the same after that. "And they were astonished at his teaching, for he taught them as one who had authority, and not as the scribes [Mark 1:22]."

THE PRIMACY OF THE KINGDOM

It was not a long ministry. It may have lasted as much as three years or as little as one. How long is not important. What is important is how the time was filled with teaching that "had authority." What was this teaching? It was many things. Yet at the heart of it, whether by the side of a lake in Galilee or in the temple of Jerusalem, there was one central theme that rang like a great bell throughout his teaching: the kingdom of God. He proclaimed it; he taught it; he held it before people; he urged them to accept it. What he said and what he did had to do with the kingdom. From the very beginning of his ministry this was so, as the Gospel of Mark does not hesitate to tell us: "Now after John was arrested, Jesus came into Galilee, preaching the gospel of God, and saying, 'The time is fulfilled, and the kingdom of God is at hand; repent, and believe in the gospel [Mark 1:14–15].'"

What did Jesus mean when he spoke of the kingdom of God? For one thing, he meant something quite different from the idea that was in the minds of his listeners. The Jewish people had for years harbored a hope for the great new kingdom that was to come. This was linked with their longing for a Messiah, a deliverer. When they thought of God's kingdom, it was a political and geographic thing. Jerusalem would be the capital of that kingdom, and God's special envoy, the Messiah, would reign supreme there. All of Israel's enemies would be crushed underfoot, and the wonderful day of prosperity and peace would come to holy Zion. For generations the people had been looking for this Messiah who would come to release them from their bondage, as Moses had done so long ago. The Messiah's coming would usher in a new day of glory for Israel.

A New Kind of Kingdom

When Jesus came it was not this kind of kingdom he had in mind. Far from it. His idea of the kingdom was so far removed from that which his people expected that they refused to accept it. As we read in the Gospels what Jesus had to say about the kingdom of God we find at least three key thoughts.

First of all, the kingdom did not refer to a geographic place. By the kingdom of God, Jesus meant the rule of God in the hearts and lives of persons. He referred to a close relationship of love and trust between God and people. When persons accept with all their heart, mind, soul and strength the authority of God over their lives they are already living within that kingdom. For the kingdom of God is a way of life lived in closeness with God.

So, the kingdom is really a matter of the heart, of how a person feels deep inside. This is why Jesus called on people to "repent and believe." He was asking them to change the whole direction of their lives, to turn around (which is what repent means) and honestly desire God's will for their lives. The idea of the kingdom is, of course, at the very center of our understanding of the New Covenant. For the New Covenant is not primarily a matter of obedience to rules and regulations but it is rather a matter of the heart, of an inward desire to follow God's will.

As important as the above understanding is, it is not enough merely to speak of the kingdom of God as the reign of God in the hearts of persons. We must see evidence of it in the world. Therefore, the kingdom means also the rule of God between and among persons. It means a new sense of compassion among people for one another. It means a wholesale change in the standards and practices of society. Jesus ardently believed this and during his entire ministry he prayed for this; he worked for this; and finally he died for this. Jesus himself was the living example of the kind of change this would mean. In his day it was regarded as very bad taste for a person to associate with others considered by society to be on a lower level. Tax collectors (who worked for hated Rome) and sinners (who had committed some obvious wrongs) were in that category. They were the outcasts of society. Did Jesus ignore them? On the contrary, he went out of his way to be with them, to talk with them, and to eat with them. Because he did so, he came under scathing attack by the Pharisees. But this did not disturb Jesus. He knew that many prejudices and unfair ways of treating people would have to be overturned in a society directed by the rule of God. Such unfair ways of treating people could have no place in the kingdom of God. Jesus pursued his ministry convinced that God's rule could come into human life and that society could be transformed. So he spoke of the kingdom that "is at hand" and compared it to a seed whose growth nothing whatever could stop (Mark 4:30–32). He told the disciples that they would see the kingdom come with power.

Finally, the kingdom of God was thought of by Jesus as that which already existed eternally. God is everlasting and so is the kingdom. While it should come upon the earth and in some measure does, it is not dependent for its existence upon our human scene. The kingdom in its fullness is that realm of life where the rule of God is most complete. We do not know much about this aspect of the kingdom. To a large extent it is hidden from our eyes. Yet we know it is very real, perhaps the most real thing of all. Jesus himself made reference to it as he ate his last meal on earth with his disciples. After they had broken bread together and had drunk the wine, he said to them: "Truly, I say to you, I shall not drink again of the fruit of the vine until that day when I drink it new in the kingdom of God [Mark 14:25]."

So Jesus came teaching. He told people the good news of a loving God who desired only their childlike trust. Let them accept God's will for their lives, and the kingdom would come in power into their lives and into the life of their nation. The kingdom was at hand. It was right there, waiting to be entered. In his teaching Jesus held this kingdom before the eyes of people, all the while looking for its coming into society.

When we think of Jesus' teaching, two things stand out: the Sermon on the Mount and his many parables. Let us take a closer look at both to see what each has to tell us.

THE SERMON ON THE MOUNT

The Sermon on the Mount comprises chapter 5, 6, and 7 of the Gospel of Matthew and chapter 6 and parts of chapters 11, 12, 13, 14, and 16 of the Gospel of Luke. We know, of course, that Jesus did not sit down one day and utter all the various teachings that now come under the heading of the Sermon on the Mount. The Sermon on the Mount is actually a collection of Jesus' teachings taken from different times and places and put together in this section by the author of the Gospel of Matthew. How are we to think of the teachings that we find there? Are they a new set of laws for Christians, meant to replace the laws we find in the Old Testament? To this, the answer is a definite no. Jesus himself said that he did not come to destroy the law and the prophets, but to fulfill them.

Certainly to understand Jesus' teachings as other kinds of laws would be to miss the whole point of the New Covenant. The New Covenant is based on a person's wanting to follow the kind of life revealed by Jesus.

Nevertheless, the teachings of the Sermon on the Mount are not to be watered down to the point where they mean nothing to us. Some people have said that these teachings of Jesus are too hard, that no one could possibly keep them. So they try to find all kinds of excuses for not following them. Even though they are not to be thought of as another kind of law, they are not meant to be ignored either.

PRINCIPLES FOR LIVING

It is probably best if we think of these teachings of Jesus as principles for living meant to guide us through the various situations we meet day by day. They are the principles that a person who accepts the rule of God over his or her life would want to live by. Beginning with the beautiful and demanding Beatitudes in Matthew 5:3–11 and ending with the story of the two men who built their houses on sand and on rock respectively, these chapters give every Christian much food for thought. Perhaps it would be helpful to take one of Jesus' teachings that we find in this collection in order to get an idea just how they are meant to apply to us. The following injunction has been a problem for generations of Christians.

> You have heard that it was said, "An eye for an eye and a tooth for a tooth." But I say to you, Do not resist one who is evil. But if any one strikes you on the right cheek, turn to him the other also; and if any one would sue you and take your coat, let him have your cloak as well; and if any one forces you to go one mile, go with him two miles. Give to him who begs from you, and do not refuse him who would borrow from you.
>
> —Matthew 5:38–42

Turning the cheek, giving up the cloak as well as the coat, going two miles instead of one, and showing complete generosity are the examples Jesus uses here to illustrate his principle. He could have used many others. So could we from our own day. The question is: What point is Jesus endeavoring to drive home to us? Is it not this? Those who have accepted the rule of God in their lives will not act in a revengeful way or carry with them revengeful attitudes. Rather, their desire in all things will be to do only that which is good and helpful and beneficial to another. The primary question then is not how many injustices happen to you; the primary question is: How does a citizen of the kingdom act? Jesus' answer is that a citizen of the kingdom acts for the welfare of others in everyting he or she does.

When one looks at the teachings that are included in the Sermon on the

Mount from the perspective of the kingdom, they begin to make a lot more sense. For these teachings are meant to be guideposts along the way for those seeking to put God and God's will at the center of their lives. To those who have no such desire, these teachings of Jesus will seem impossible. But others will continue to do the best they can to follow them because the teachings are right and worth their striving. Even when they fail, they know that they can count on God's help in getting back on their feet and started on the high road again. Therefore they never lose heart as they seek first God's kingdom and God's righteousness.

JESUS' USE OF PARABLES

Why did Jesus use parables? He felt that this was the best way for him to convey to people the truth about God and God's kingdom, and their relationship to God and that kingdom.

What were the parables about? This differed somewhat according to the viewpoint of the Gospel writer. The Gospel of Mark stresses the inevitable coming of the kingdom and reports Jesus' parable of the seed and its silent, relentless growth (Mark 4:26–29). The Gospel of Matthew strikes a note of judgment and reports Jesus' parable of the guests who were invited to the wedding of a king's son (Matthew 22:1–14). Those who were invited scorned the invitation and were finally punished by the king. But others were recruited from the streets and brought to the wedding feast. The parable means to point out simply that the very ones who think they are going to enter the kingdom are in for a rude awakening. It may well be that those held in the least esteem by society will be the recipients of God's grace in overflowing measure.

THE PARABLE OF THE TWO SONS

The Gospel of Luke, though containing a somewhat similar parable (14:16–24), has as one of its special marks the love and compassion of God. In this connection we find reported one of the most stirring of Jesus' parables, the parable of the two sons (15:11–32). No spoken word of Jesus has ever revealed the character of God to us so beautifully as has this.

This parable has traditionally been called the parable of the prodigal son. Actually it concerns the father and his two sons. One of the sons left home with his share of the savings. But he got in with some bad company, did some pretty foolish things, and before long both his money and his so-called friends were gone. He was desperate—so desperate that he hired himself out to a local farmer and fed pigs. But he got so little for his work that he ended up eating the pigs' food. One day he came to himself and decided to return home. He resolved to ask his father if he could be one of the servants; he no longer felt worthy of being regarded as a son. He then started home. Meanwhile the father, being a compassionate and loving father, had never stopped worrying about his son. Looking down the road one day, he saw his son coming home. The father's heart leaped for joy. With eyes clouded by tears of happiness, he rushed down the road to meet his son and embraced him.

When his son said that he no longer felt worthy of being a son and asked only for a chance to work as one of his father's servants, the father would have none of it. He ordered the servants to bring the best robe and put it on his son and to bring a ring for his finger and shoes for his feet and to kill the fatted calf so they could celebrate his son's return. The father explained his reasons for doing all this by saying, "This my son was dead, and is alive again; he was lost, and is found."

As soon as the older son heard of this, he became angry with his father. He had served his father for many years, had been loyal and obedient, and had not made a fool of himself. But he had never been treated like this! At that his father must have put his arm around him and reminded him that everything he had belonged to him. He loved him just as much as his runaway son. But it was proper to celebrate the return of a son who they thought was dead.

The picture of a father waiting expectantly for his child to return to him that he might forgive him, while at the same time loving the child who was obedient to him—such a word picture tells us volumes about the nature of the loving God whom Jesus revealed to people.

It is little wonder that the common people heard Jesus gladly. He spoke in their language; he spoke of things they knew. And when he spoke, there were stirrings of the soul that people had not felt before. Truly, a prophet had arisen in their midst. Yet he was more than a prophet.

Scene 4.
COMPASSION

Jesus, James, John, and Peter had been absent from the rest of the disciples for a time. Now all four of them were returning. Up ahead of them they could see that a large crowd of people had gathered. The crowd shifted back and forth slightly according to what was happening in the middle of it. As they drew nearer they heard anguished groans and yells. The four stepped up their pace as they hurried to see what was happening. Just then some of the crowd caught sight of Jesus and came running toward him. A man was the first to speak. The tone of his voice and the anguish of his face left no doubt that whatever was going on involved him. He said: "Teacher, I brought my son to you, for he has a dumb spirit; and wherever it seizes him, it dashes him down; and he foams and grinds his

140

teeth and becomes rigid; and I asked your disciples to cast it out, and they were not able [Mark 9:17–18]."

When he heard the report, Jesus was visibly disturbed and asked that the boy be brought to him immediately. It was not a pretty sight. The youngster rolled on the ground uttering strange sounds and foaming at the mouth. "Jesus asked his father, 'How long has he had this?' And he said, 'From childhood. And it has often cast him into the fire and into the water, to destroy him; but if you can do anything, have pity on us and help us [Mark 9:21–22].'"

"If you can!" Jesus was taken aback by the father's evident lack of faith. "All things are possible to him who believes."

Immediately the child's father cried out as if in desperation, "I believe; help my unbelief!" Then Jesus spoke again, "You dumb and deaf spirit, I command you, come out of him, and never enter him again." One final convulsion, one final cry, and the boy was still—so still that some thought he was dead. But Jesus took him by the hand, helped him to his feet, and sent him on his way with his father. Yet something troubled the disciples. Why could they not cure the boy? So they asked Jesus the question. Jesus answered, "This kind cannot be driven out by anything but prayer."

MIRACLES IN THE NEW TESTAMENT

What can be said about the miraculous element that enters into this story and into many other parts of the New Testament? In the first place, the authors of the Gospels recorded reports of incidents that had come to them from the fund of knowledge about Jesus that existed in the early Christian community. They were reporters who set down accounts that have been given to them by others. In some cases, they may have been eyewitnesses. Whatever we may or may not think about a particular incident is, in a sense, not too important. Whether we like it or not, we had before us what someone of the early church claims to have witnessed, or claims that someone else witnessed. Whatever the case, something mighty important happened—important enough to be remembered. If it was that important, then we had better take stock of it.

Second, miracles for the people of Jesus' day were not the problem they are to us today. As far as they were concerned, this was just the way God chose to operate at a particular time through a particular person who stood in special relationship to God. They knew very little about the healing processes or the constitution of the body and mind. When they saw a boy who was caught up in violent convulsions and who foamed at the mouth, they said that he had a demon or an unclean spirit. Today we would call this disease epilepsy and would prescribe appropriate treatment. But the people of the first century A.D. lived in a prescientific age and knew nothing of this illness, its causes, or its cure. A miracle was to

141

them a very wonderful thing, an act of God. But it was entirely believable, with none of the reservations we would tend to have today.

In the third place, one would have to admit that in the course of being handed down from one generation to another, exaggerations of the original accounts could have occurred. All we have to do is to consider the various legends that have arisen already about men like George Washington and Abraham Lincoln to see the truth of this.

Fourth, we are on the wrong track if our concern is always for *how* a particular miracle occurred. It is all too easy to get wrapped up in the mechanics of a reported miracle and overlook the truth that it is attempting to convey. To put it another way, the miracles in the biblical account ought to be looked at for the religious message they have to offer us.

Fifth, we must remember that miracles were not performed by Jesus as signs of his divinity or merely for the purpose of drawing a crowd. These mighty acts were the result of the power of the kingdom of God at work through Jesus. The power of God in Jesus met sickness in persons and, in ways mostly unknown to us, transformed illness into health. Physicians, psychiatrists, and ministers work together today to accomplish some of these same wonderful transformations in people.

Finally, it is well to remember that the greatest miracle was Jesus' incarnation and resurrection. The eternal Word put on mortal flesh and dwelt among us. God became human. He who was put to death so cruelly on a cross because he loved us so much was also raised from the dead as the sign that the power of life can conquer the power of death and that the power of love can conquer the power of hate. This was the greatest miracle. All other "miracles" pale into comparative insignificance before that.

FAITH AND PRAYER

Up to this point we have laid down some general principles to bear in mind when coming face to face with miracle stories. But what about individual incidents? We have already considered demon possession or what we would have called epilepsy, a chronic disease of the nervous system. Here we see not only the great compassion of Jesus but also his ability to effect a cure by making himself a channel of God's healing power. We see also the part played by the faith of the father. It is interesting to note that the cure became possible after the father in utter sincerity shouted, "I believe; help my unbelief!" Jesus gave us another insight into the situation when he said, "This kind cannot be driven out by anything but prayer." By this Jesus did not mean a specific prayer. He was referring rather to that kind of close association between himself and God. It was this that made it possible for him to effect such healing.

THE FEEDING OF THE FIVE THOUSAND

Now let us turn to a different kind of miracle, the feeding of the five thousand. The disciples had just returned from a special preaching mission, and Jesus wished to be alone with them. Then, too, John had just been beheaded by the murderous Herod. This must have weighed heavily on Jesus' heart. So being by the shore of the Sea of Galilee, they got into a boat and went off to a spot where they supposed they could be alone. But it was not to be. Many of the people saw them and hurried on foot to the same spot they were heading for by boat. There were people waiting for him when Jesus arrived. What was Jesus' reaction to this infringement of his privacy? "As he went ashore he saw a great throng, and he had compassion on them, because they were like sheep without a shepherd; and he began to teach them many things [Mark 6:34]."

When it grew late the disciples suggested to the Master that he send the people away to the villages so they could get something to eat. Jesus' answer to them caught them by surprise. He said, "You give them something to eat." Then the disciples wanted to know if he meant that they should buy two hundred denarii (one denarius was an average wage for a day's labor) worth of bread and give the bread to the people to eat.

But Jesus did not mean this. Instead he used the five loaves and two fishes already on hand. He asked the people to sit down on the grass. Then taking the loaves and the fish, he looked up to heaven, blessed them, and gave them to the disciples to set before the crowd. Everyone ate and was satisfied. There were about five thousand—in some accounts, four thousand—men, not counting women and children, fed in all. Many baskets of broken pieces of bread and fish were left over.

This incident has been interpreted in different ways. Some have said that the whole thing was really symbolic, meaning to indicate that Jesus gave people the spiritual bread of life. Others have said that the reason everyone was fed and there was much left over was because those who had something shared with those who had nothing. One thing, however, is certain. The author of the Gospel of Mark considered the story of the multiplication of the fish and loaves as a miracle. There was no attempt whatever to explain it away or detract from its wonder. That was the story as it came to him, and he passed it on to his readers. It is probably best if we do the same thing. Rather than get lost in trying to explain something which is completely impossible to explain, we might better ask the question: What did this event mean to Jesus?

Again it seems to be linked closely with the idea of the kingdom, which was central in Jesus' witness. Jesus had run into opposition in his witness to the kingdom. Nevertheless, he still held firmly to the belief that the kingdom was at hand.

One of the symbols of the kingdom for the Jewish people was that of a great banquet. Could the meal shared by Jesus with the throng on a Galilean hillside be his own testimony to the fact that the kingdom would come? Many feel that this is the real meaning of this episode in the life of Jesus.

The miracles of Jesus were not demonstrations of power for its own sake. Rather, they were a continuous witness to the fact that in Jesus of Nazareth the kingdom of God was present among people. They were signs of the New Covenant that God had created. In Jesus God lived among people and helped them when they could not help themselves. The power of God's goodness met the sickness in their lives and changed them, making them whole and well. This Jesus did for a comparatively few people in a tiny part of the world of that day. But already it was a promise of what God would do for all those who trusted in the Creator, who laid their lives at God's feet.

Jesus placed his hand on a fevered brow or on a sick soul and gave peace and new meaning to life. Yet in that same moment he was giving the promise of peace and new meaning to life for all people who would trust in God. Here is the joy, here is the wonder of the New Covenant. Jesus presents us with the opportunity to live in closer fellowship with God and so discover the life that is life indeed. All we need to do is say in word, in deed, in intention, "I believe." Perhaps, after all, this is the real miracle.

Scene 5.
THE BLINDING SUNBURST

A TIME OF RETREAT

There came a time in the ministry of Jesus when he found that he must go off somewhere all alone for a period. At the beginning of his ministry he had taken time to think through some basic questions. Once again he had some deep thinking to do. Why? Because during his ministry he had witnessed no great change of heart on the part of the people, and consequently no invasion of the kingdom of God into their hearts and lives and nation. He had worked and prayed ceaselessly that this would take place. He preached, he taught, he healed; and everything was done to the end that people would repent and turn to God.

Perhaps he had been successful as the world counts success. The common people gladly listened to the words of wisdom that came from his lips. And the sick and the diseased worshiped him for making them well. He was popular among the people; his name was known throughout the nation. Indeed, Jesus even suspected that the people would like to make him a king over them if he would only let them. But he had not come for that; it was the very thing he had rejected at the beginning of his ministry. He came to represent the rule of God over the lives of persons and society; he came to preach the good news of a kingdom that was near at hand; he came to call people to repentance and faith. But nothing had happened. He had been successful in everything except what he wanted most. In fact, this other kind of success was actually getting in the way of his real reason for coming.

His popularity was, however, not the only element in the picture. Hostility to him and his message was always apparent. This was provided by the religious and political leaders who had become most suspicious of his activities and who had caught the brunt of his words.

What, then, was he to do? If the people would not listen to his words, his urgings, how would they be brought to repentance and to faith? These were the questions that must have occupied Jesus during this second time of retreat near the end of his earthly ministry. He left Galilee and journeyed north to the region of Tyre and Sidon and there secluded himself.

THE GREAT CONFESSION

It was shortly after this period of retreat that we come across Jesus with his disciples in the region of Caesarea Philippi. Perhaps it was while walking across a quiet country path that Jesus asked his disciples the simple question, "Who do men say that I am?" The question called forth a variety of answers. Some said he was John the Baptist (who had been beheaded by Herod) come back to life. Others said he was Elijah (that great Old Testament prophet, whose return had been expected). Still others said one of the prophets (of whom there had been many).

Having heard the various answers proposed, Jesus then turned the question on them: "But who do you say that I am?" Peter, whether as his own spokesman or spokesman for the group, had the answer ready: "You are the Christ." In other words you are the anointed of God, God's own chosen one. This was the conviction of the small band of disciples who had left all to follow him. That they did not completely understand what this meant is clearly shown in what happened next. As soon as the great confession had been made by Peter, Jesus turned to his disciples. "And he began to teach them that the Son of man must suffer many things, and be rejected by the elders and the chief priests and the scribes, and be killed, and after three days rise again. And he said this plainly [Mark 8:31–32]."

THE ROAD OF SUFFERING

The disciples were aghast. This was incredible! Such a thing would never happen to one who was God's own anointed, God's chosen one. His would be victory and glory, not defeat and rejection. Peter was especially disturbed at this turn of events and began to scold Jesus for daring to say such things.

But this was the thought that had been coming to Jesus for a long time. This was the idea that he had worked out in his period of retreat near Tyre. The people had rejected the kingdom of God, or at least were indifferent to it. Just to proclaim it was not enough. Now he must do something that would open the hearts of the people to the kingdom and open the kingdom to people. There was only one road open—the road of suffering. He would have to take upon himself the consequences of his people's rejection of God's kingdom.

Once in his baptism he had identified himself with the people's guilt and their need for repentance. Now once again he would identify himself with his people. He who knew no sin would take upon himself the consequences of their sin. He would be offered up, if need be, as a voluntary sacrifice for their blindness. Jesus must have been thoroughly acquainted with what the prophet called Second Isaiah had to say centuries ago about the suffering of one for the sins of many. Second Isaiah had referred to Israel's suffering for the sins of all the nations of the earth. Jesus made this idea of Isaiah personal, and applied it to himself. Christians ever since have seen in this word of Second Isaiah a prophecy that seemed to speak of the sacrifice of Jesus for the sake of all people.

> He was despised and rejected by men;
>   a man of sorrows, and acquainted with grief;
> and as one from whom men hide their faces
>   he was despised, and we esteemed him not.
>
> Surely he has borne our griefs
>   and carried our sorrows;
> yet we esteemed him stricken,
>   smitten by God, and afflicted.
> But he was wounded for our transgressions,
>   he was bruised for our iniquities;
> upon him was the chastisement that made us whole,
>   and with his stripes we are healed.
>   —Isaiah 53:3–5

From proclaimer of the kingdom to the servant who would suffer for the hardness of people's hearts, Jesus had indeed walked a long road.

Events moved swiftly from this point. The Gospel of Mark records the experience of transfiguration to declare to the reader Jesus' inward authority and divine sonship. This was, no doubt, a very moving religious experience for Jesus, one that served to bolster him for the trying days ahead. Following a brief ministry on the other side of the Jordan, he came to Jerusalem and taught there about three months. Then he left for a final period of thought and meditation in the wilderness of Perea, east of

Jerusalem, moving a little later to the town of Ephraim. Here he stayed for another three months. During this time his mind must have been filled with thoughts of the almost certain death that awaited him when he returned to Jerusalem at the Passover festival.

JESUS ENTERS JERUSALEM

Jesus made his final entry into the city of Jerusalem a few days before the Passover, on what Christians now call Palm Sunday. This has often been called the triumphal entry. Yet in the mind of Jesus it was anything but that. The people who cheered him and who threw palm branches before him misunderstood why he had come. They were looking for a military messiah who would deliver them from political and economic oppression. Jesus purposely rode into Jerusalem on a donkey, a symbol of a man of peace. But the crowd would have none of it. They hailed him as a conqueror, a mighty leader, the long awaited Messiah who would come with his heavenly armies and rout the foe. This was not really a day of rejoicing for Jesus. It was the beginning of the tragedy that was soon to follow. If he had held to any hope that the people's ideas might change and that they might yet receive the message of the kind of kingdom he came to proclaim, that hope was firmly and thoroughly dashed to pieces in that hour.

The events of the last days of his life moved even more quickly. Judas, one of the Twelve, seeing no hopes of gain in the company of Jesus, offered his services to the chief priests who were trying to get rid of Jesus. They felt that he was a threat to their position. A bargain was made. At the proper time Judas was to betray the Master into their hands with a kiss. The Gospel of Matthew reports that the fee paid Judas was thirty pieces of silver.

THE LAST SUPPER

Right after that strange incident, Jesus shared his last meal with his disciples. This must have occurred on a Thursday evening. Following careful preparation, the disciples came together with the Master. The heart of their fellowship meal is described for us in the following brief account:

> And as they were eating, he took bread, and blessed, and broke it, and gave it to them, and said, "Take; this is my body." And he took a cup, and when he had given thanks he gave it to them, and they all drank of it. And he said to them, "This is my blood of the covenant, which is poured out for many. Truly, I say to you, I shall not drink again of the fruit of the vine until that day when I drink it new in the kingdom of God."
>
> —Mark 14:22–25

147

The spirit of this meal, though not necessarily one of despondency, could hardly have been one of gaiety. The disciples were not blind. They had feelings, and they could not have helped sensing what was happening in Jerusalem as each day passed. The antagonism of the religious authorities to Jesus was evident. There was an undercurrent of unrest among the people too. Jesus had made no great move after his acclamation that occurred when he entered the city a few days before. It was clear to all by now that Jesus was not going to accept the hero role they had accorded him.

Jesus sat at the table with his little band of men. He had often sat with them so. At times like this and on many other occasions he spoke to them of the things that were in his mind and on his heart. He hoped that he had taught them well. But was his teaching enough? Did they need something else, something that would bind them to him in the days ahead? This was the last time they would be together, this was the *last* supper. If there were something else to be done, it must be done now.

THE BLOOD OF THE COVENANT

So he took the bread that was before him on the table, broke it before their eyes, and passed it on to them. The bread was a symbol of his own body that was about to be "broken" on a cross. The disciples in taking the bread were pledging themselves to suffer with and for Christ in his service. Then he took the cup of wine, sipped from it himself, and passed it on to the disciples. The wine represented his life blood about to be shed. He called it the "blood of the covenant." This was his pledge to his disciples that even as they would share in his suffering, so they would share in the new life and joy of the kingdom which his sacrifice would bring near to all people.

One wonders as Jesus did this if his thoughts traveled back through the centuries to another scene. Do you remember it? A great throng of people gathered at the foot of a smoking, thundering mountain. Before them the towering figure of Moses was standing beside a crude altar. In his hands was a basin with the blood of an animal that had just been sacrificed. Half the blood he threw against the altar; half he threw over the heads of the people. From his mouth rang the declaration, "Behold the blood of the covenant which the Lord has made with you in accordance with all these words" [Exod. 24:8]."

At that unforgettable supper with his disciples, Jesus referred to something more than the blood of an animal. "This is *my* blood of the covenant," he said. And so it would be. His was to be the blood of a *New* Covenant to *all* people. The blood that was shed on Golgotha's hill would sweep like a mighty river through Palestine, into Asia Minor, up through Europe, and into every corner of the earth. As it went it would catch people up in its torrent until they, too, learned of a God who loved them, who was near to them, and who gave them the power needed for redemptive, joyful, and servant-like living. To start this river of the saving grace of God on its way required a mighty deed. This Jesus already knew. To this deed he had already committed himself.

TRIAL AND CRUCIFIXION

Jesus left the upper room with his disciples, made his way across the Kidron brook just outside Jerusalem to the Mount of Olives, and struggled fiercely in the agony of prayer. It was not easy for Jesus to go voluntarily to death. "Let this cup [of suffering] pass from me," he prayed. But he added, "nevertheless not my will, but thine, be done." And before his betrayer ascended the hill, he was serenely prepared for what must come.

Judas and the soldiers of the chief priests came and took him prisoner after he was pointed out to them by the fateful kiss. There followed the ignominy of trials before the Jewish Sanhedrin and before Pilate, the Roman governor. Trumped up charges were leveled against Jesus by bribed witnesses. He was accused of making himself out to be divine and of wanting to be king. Pilate did not think very much of the charges; he did not believe that Jesus deserved death as a penalty. However, the chief priests were insistent. They stirred up the people to shout for Jesus' death. When given the choice of Jesus or Barabbas, who had a long record of troublemaking, they shouted for the latter to be released to them and for Jesus to be crucified. Barabbas was set free, and Jesus was delivered to the soldiers who mocked and beat him.

Finally he was taken from the guardhouse, given a heavy cross to carry, and led through the city streets toward a hill called Golgotha, "the place of a skull." Tradition has given us the story that one called Simon of Cyrene carried Jesus' cross for him. All too quickly they arrived at the dreaded place. The New Testament reports in Mark 15:24 the next event in these blunt words: "And they crucified him."

It was about nine o'clock in the morning when they crucified Jesus. He hung on the cross for six hours, or until three o'clock in the afternoon. The day was Friday. On either side of him was a robber being crucified also. Beneath him was a taunting mob that had followed the condemned men to the hill of crucifixion. In the midst of enduring the cruel pain and ignominy of such a death, Jesus had to bear also the insults and barbed taunts of a jeering crowd. Christian tradition has recorded in the four Gospels a total of seven key words or phrases that came from the lips of Jesus during this time on the cross. Of the seven, three are particularly revealing.

WORDS FROM A CROSS

"Father, forgive them; for they know not what they do." These words of Jesus recorded in Luke 23:34 speak volumes of his intense love for persons, even while they taunted him. All the hate and cruelty they could throw at him did not cause him to respond in kind. Instead he took it, transformed it, and hurled it back at them as a word of forgiving love. How great a love he had!

"My God, my God, why hast thou forsaken me?" These words recorded in Mark 15:34 remind us of the intense humanity of Jesus. He was human even as we are human. He really suffered all the agonies of one so cruelly put to death. Although the Son of God, he experienced the awful, terrifying feeling of being cut off from God, even if for only a fleeting moment.

"Father, into thy hands I commit my spirit!" Here in Luke 23:46 is the final expression of complete confidence in God and God's will. It was a confidence that characterized Jesus' life. He had given himself into the hands of God all the days of his ministry and in the last trying days as well.

Having said this, he breathed his last. A few sorrowing women heard his cry and a Roman guard, looking up in astonishment, cried: "Truly this man was a Son of God [Mark 15:39]!"

It is no accident that the cross is central in a Christian service of worship. Many churches have placed it on the altar or above the altar, or perhaps in a huge stained glass window behind the altar. When people have looked at that cross, they have seen more than the terrible consequences of hatred, jealousy, and pride. They have seen also that which has overcome and trampled these sins underfoot—the forgiving love of God that shone through Jesus the crucified. Never have the heights or depths of God's love been more clearly revealed than there. Never has the power of God's love in human life stood out so transparently. Glimpses of it were seen here and there in the Old Covenant story. But now it exploded as a full sunburst upon the world.

The meaning of this event was not at first apparent to all. Following Jesus' death, there was only deep sorrow and despair. Those who loved Jesus felt overwhelmed by the tragedy that cut short his life. But what sense was there to it now? What sense was there to all the things he had told them, to all the things he did? There was real darkness in the souls of those who had loved him; but it was a darkness that served only to make more blinding the light that dawned a few days later.

RESURRECTION

Jesus was not dead! He was alive. He was with them. They knew not how, nor did they seem to care how. It was a mystery to them, hidden in the will and action of God. But Jesus had risen from the dead and had appeared to them. He had been experienced by them. Of this, they were absolutely sure. To this mighty event the four Gospels give witness, each in its own way, some more thoroughly than others. To this fact, the early preaching of the apostles gives witness. Indeed, it is the cornerstone of their preaching, as it is the cornerstone of their faith. And to this event Paul gives witness when he states:

> For I delivered to you as of first importance what I also received, that Christ died for our sins in accordance with the scriptures, that he was buried, that he was raised on the third day in accordance with the scriptures, and that he appeared to Cephas, then to the twelve. Then he appeared to more than five hundred brethren at one time, most of whom are still alive, though some have fallen asleep. Then he appeared to James, then to all the apostles. Last of all, as to one untimely born, he appeared also to me.
> —1 Corinthians 15:3–8

How did it happen? What kind of body did Jesus have? How could he be seen by the disciples? To these questions we have no final answers. But these are not the most important questions. Evidently the biblical writers, or the early apostles, did not consider them important enough to require specific answers. They were too caught up in the joy of Jesus' resurrection to be concerned about the how of it. But the church, the whole church in all lands and in all ages, is the living proof of the fact that Jesus is alive. Without the resurrection there would be no church. Without the resurrection there would have been no good news to proclaim, or any power with which to proclaim it. It was the resurrection of Jesus and the Holy Spirit entering in power into the lives of the disciples that changed them from a group of dejected and confused men into champions of the Christian gospel and founders of the Christian church. Nothing less could have accomplished it. Nothing more was needed.

The accounts of Jesus' resurrection appearances as we have them in the New Testament have come to us from the traditions of the early church. It is important to look at these stories not as the product of a newspaper reporter who was on hand with paper and pencil when they happened. If there had been such a reporter present, that reporter probably would have seen nothing and experienced nothing. For the resurrected Jesus is not so much seen by the physical eye as he is "seen" by the eye of faith. The stories of Jesus' resurrection appearances come from the devotion of the Christian community. They are not meant to convey cold historical fact, but saving religious meaning. It is in that light that they must be appreciated.

THE TWOFOLD EVENT

The crucifixion and resurrection of Jesus Christ is the twofold event that must be seen as one brilliant sunburst upon a darkened world. In his death Jesus became the sacrifice for our sins, without which the New Covenant would not have been possible. Without that sacrifice, we would not have seen the tragic consequences of the sin deep in each of us or God's tremendous love for us that is able to overcome our sin. But having seen that love, we feel drawn to it.

In his resurrection, Jesus became our pledge that we too can live in an eternal sense. That is, we have the possibility of living here and now through the power of the Holy Spirit. This power makes our lives meaningful, redemptive, helpful, joyous, and purposeful. And when our short journey on earth is finished, we shall continue to live such lives ever more fully in eternal fellowship with God. To live in such a way—to live believing that in all things and in every situation, God is present in power and in love—this is to live as a child of the New Covenant. Look for one who lives life in fear and you will see one who knows nothing of this. But hear another singing a song in the midst of trouble and you will see a child of the covenant.

A NEW RELATIONSHIP

The New Covenant brought a new relationship between God and ourselves. God's love for us was thenceforth to be met by our trust. But more. God, through the Holy Spirit, would work in the hearts and lives of people to help them trust. So, in the New Covenant, God not only works from the Divine side, God works from our side too. This is the joy of it; this is the wonder of it. Read again the parable of the two sons in Luke and it may help you to understand this better.

The New Covenant meant also a new relationship between persons. As Christians we believe God can work where and when God chooses. Yet we know that already, in Jesus, God was fashioning a communion of persons who would carry this good news to the world. This communion was destined to grow and to become known as the Christian church. From the very beginning, the New Covenant was meant to be lived in communion with other persons. Indeed, it is in communion with others that the New Covenant takes on meaning for our lives. We cannot very well talk of loving God if we do not love one another. If God's love is in our lives, we will want to share it. With others of the Christian communion, we will want to work to bring it to those who have not heard such good news for their lives.

It was Jesus' crucifixion and resurrection that made him Lord for the early apostles. Of this they ceaselessly spoke; to this they constantly gave witness. It was this that catapulted them into the New Covenant and made them courageous champions of the good news of God. The whole life of Jesus, and indeed, the whole plan of God through the history of the

Israelite nation, was seen as receiving its culmination in this mighty act of God. Here was the climax of the drama of salvation. Here was God entering into history in a way that completely changed the world. An empty cross stands as a symbol for all time of God's having come to earth to reach out to us. All that we have to do is to reach out and be led.

THE STORY OF THE EARLY CHURCH

Scene 1.
A FAITH THAT WAS CONTAGIOUS

Pentecost has always been regarded by Christians as the birth date of the Christian church. Acts, our source book for early church history, reports that on this day the Holy Spirit came with power upon the apostles. Filled with the Holy Spirit, they went out into the business district of the city at the time of a high festival and boldly proclaimed Jesus to be the Savior of the world. So affected were many by the testimony of these men and the working of the Holy Spirit that the record states (Acts 2:41): "So those who received his word were baptized, and there were added that day about three thousand souls."

The good news of the New Covenant spread far and wide. Those who were filled with it themselves felt that they had to share it with others, whatever the consequences. Initially the church was quite small. Early Christians met first in one another's homes. And being Jews, as these first converts were, they did not stop going to the temple and synagogue to attend the regular services to which they were accustomed. After all, Jesus had said that he did not come "to abolish the law and the prophets . . . but to fulfill them." They saw nothing amiss in attending the temple services as well as meeting in one another's homes. There is an interesting description of this earliest Christian community in the books of Acts:

And fear came upon every soul; and many wonders and signs were done through the apostles. And all who believed were together and had all things in common; and they sold their possessions and goods and distributed them to all, as any had need. And day by day, attending the temple together and breaking bread in their homes, they partook of food with glad and generous hearts, praising God and having favor with all the people. And the Lord added to their number day by day those who were being saved.

—Acts 2:43–47

155

COURAGEOUS WITNESS

Many virtues marked these early Christians. Perhaps the greatest was their courage, courage born of the Holy Spirit. No matter how they were threatened, they refused to keep silent. One day Peter and John were speaking to people about Jesus and telling them how God had raised him from the dead. They were immediately arrested by the religious authorities and thrown in jail. The next day the authorities held a council and put Peter and John in the middle of them.

"By what power or by what name did you do this?" they demanded. By "this" they meant an act of healing that Peter had performed on a man over forty years old who could not walk. The scripture reports Peter's answer as follows:

> Rulers of the people and elders, if we are being examined today concerning a good deed done to a cripple, by what means this man has been healed, be it known to you all, and to all the people of Israel, that by the name of Jesus Christ of Nazareth, whom you crucified, whom God raised from the dead, by him this man is standing before you well. This is the stone which was rejected by you builders, but which has become the head of the corner. And there is salvation in no one else, for there is no other name under heaven given among men by which we must be saved.
>
> —Acts 4:8–12

The council told them that for their own good they had better stop preaching and teaching such things. Peter's answer to this threat is classic: "Whether it is right in the sight of God to listen to you rather than to God, you must judge; for we cannot but speak of what we have seen and heard [Acts 4:19–20]."

STEPHEN: FIRST CHRISTIAN MARTYR

The apostles were arrested more than once; they were beaten and warned to keep their mouths shut. But this did not deter them. They had a gospel to preach and nothing on earth was going to stop them. One of the finest examples of courage and devotion that has come down to us from the annals of early church history concerns one who was not of the original apostles, a man by the name of Stephen. Stephen was one of seven men chosen by the apostles to help take care of the physical needs of some of the members of the fellowship. His witness to his faith was apparently too strong, for it came to the attention of the rulers of the synagogue. Charges were made against him that he spoke "blasphemous words against Moses and God" and that he had said: "Jesus of Nazareth will destroy this place [the temple] and will change the customs which Moses delivered to us." Stephen was then given an opportunity to make his defense.

His speech covers the whole of chapter 7 in the book of Acts. It consists of a rehearsal of the history of the Hebrew nation in which he showed how the people had turned from the worship of the true God even in the days of Moses. Then he concluded his speech by saying:

> You stiff-necked people, uncircumcised in heart and ears, you always resist the Holy Spirit. As your fathers did, so do you. Which of the prophets did not your fathers persecute? And they killed those who announced beforehand the coming of the Righteous One, whom you have now betrayed and murdered, you who received the law as delivered by angels and did not keep it.
>
> —Acts 7:51–53

How do you think his listeners took to these words of Stephen? To say that they were angry is to put it mildly. The scripture says, "They were enraged, and they ground their teeth against him." They grabbed hold of him, took him out of the city, and set him against the wall. There they stoned him to death. Before he died, "he knelt down and cried with a loud voice, 'Lord, do not hold this sin against them.' And when he had said this, he fell asleep. And Saul was consenting to his death [Acts 7:60–8:1]."

It took real courage to bear a Christian witness in the early days of the church. The church was in the minority in a hostile environment. It would have been much safer for its members to keep quiet. But that was the one thing that Christians could not do. They had good news to tell, a covenant to share, and they simply had to share it with others.

CORNELIUS: FIRST GENTILE CHRISTIAN

At the beginning, the church was a Jewish church. This was natural since the Christian faith had its beginning in Jewish surroundings. There is, however, an interesting story in Acts that tells us that very early a problem arose for these first Jewish Christian leaders. A non-Jewish family wanted to become Christian. What to do? The family in question was that of Cornelius, a Roman centurion. His story is found in chapter 10 of Acts. He was stationed at the town of Caesarea, "a devout man who feared God with all his household, gave alms liberally to the people, and prayed constantly to God." This man desired to be baptized into the Christian faith. In a vision he was told to send for Peter, and he immediately dispatched two servants and one of his soldiers to fetch him. Meanwhile Peter had a disturbing dream in which he was bidden to eat certain kinds of food which, as a loyal Jew, he considered to be unclean. Then the voice of God spoke to him saying, "What God has cleansed, you must not call common." When the messengers from Cornelius arrived and stated their business, Peter agreed to go with them. He arrived at Caesarea and went to the home of Cornelius. He told Cornelius about the vision that he had

had and how it had taught him that he was not to call anyone common or unclean. Peter then confessed his faith, a confession which had as its center Jesus' crucifixion and resurrection. What interests us most at this point, however, is the way in which he began his witness. He affirmed (Acts 10:34–35): "Truly I perceive that God shows no partiality, but in every nation any one who fears him and does what is right is acceptable to him."

While Peter spoke, "the Holy Spirit fell on all who heard the word." A few Jewish Christians were present when the power of the Holy Spirit came upon the household of Cornelius.

"Can any one forbid water for baptizing these people who have received the Holy Spirit just as we have?" asked Peter. The answer was obvious. No one dared to forbid it. Thereupon Cornelius and his family were baptized into the Christian faith. They represented the first gentiles to enter the Christian faith. This was a very big step for the early Jewish Christians. It was an admission by the Jewish Christians that a person could become a Christian without having first to conform to certain Jewish laws and customs. Many Jewish Christians would hesitate before they finally accepted this. But eventually it became an official policy of the church.

The church continued to grow in spite of persecution—or maybe because of it. There was a close spiritual kinship among these early Christians that many modern Christians envy. Theirs was a real communion of heart, mind, and soul. Their fellowship ran deep. Each one lived for the welfare of the whole. This is evident from the description of their life that is recorded in the book of Acts. They owned no private property but gave it all for the welfare of the community. No one was in need; all shared alike within the community. Thus, mention is made of a certain Barnabas who "sold a field which belonged to him, and brought the money and laid it at the apostles' feet [Acts 4:37]."

Here were people of the New Covenant, guided by the Holy Spirit, who were living in a relationship of love and trust with God and with one another. This relationship was the basis of their life together, the binding force of their community.

Scene 2.

A MAN NAMED PAUL

SAUL: THE PERSECUTOR

Anyone watching the early performance of that watchdog of the Pharisees named Saul would have given him the title of "least likely candidate to become a Christian." And with good reason. Born of Jewish parents in the town of Tarsus on the southern coast of Asia Minor, Saul was then living in

Jerusalem. As a boy he was schooled in the Law of the Jewish religion. He was a young man with a keen mind and a ready enthusiasm, so he learned quickly. In order to learn more, he came to Jerusalem and studied under the great Jewish scholar Gamaliel. The more he studied, the greater became his fascination and zeal for the Law of his Jewish faith. So it was with utter contempt that he heard of the new sect whose members babbled about a Christ who was the true Messiah. He determined to do all he could to wipe out the new sect.

Saul had been a witness to the death of Stephen outside the walls of Jerusalem. What impression this made on him we do not know. Certainly it was of no immediate help to the Christian cause. Stephen's death was the signal for a general outbreak of persecution against the Christians in Jerusalem. The persecution was so violent that many of the Christians fled to other cities and regions. Saul himself was in the vanguard of this particular wave. The scripture reports (Acts 8:3): "But Saul was ravaging the church, and entering house after house, he dragged off men and women and committed them to prison."

His zeal against the adherents of this new "Way" led to his being given letters to the synagogues at Damascus. If he should find any followers of the Way there, he was to bring them back to Jerusalem. With the thought of routing more Christians out of their homes in Damascus, he journeyed toward that city. However something happened on that journey that changed the course of his entire life. The scriptural account tells it best:

> Now as he journeyed he approached Damascus, and suddenly a light from heaven flashed about him. And he fell to the ground and heard a voice saying to him, "Saul, Saul, why do you persecute me?" And he said, "Who are you, Lord?" And he said, "I am Jesus, whom you are persecuting; but rise and enter the city, and you will be told what you are to do." The men who were traveling with him stood speechless, hearing the voice but seeing no one. Saul arose from the ground; and when his eyes were opened, he could see nothing; so they led him by the hand and brought him into Damascus. And for three days he was without sight, and neither ate nor drank.
>
> —Acts 9:3–9

PAUL: THE APOSTLE

It was the living Jesus who confronted the vengeful Saul on the road to Damascus. It was the living Jesus who took this hater of Christians and turned him into a fearless crusader for the Christian gospel. Never has there been a greater about-face than this. Saul stayed in Damascus a few days, received his sight back, and was baptized by a Christian named Ananias. Following this experience Paul felt the need for a time of retreat. He retired to the Arabian desert to be alone with his thoughts, his

159

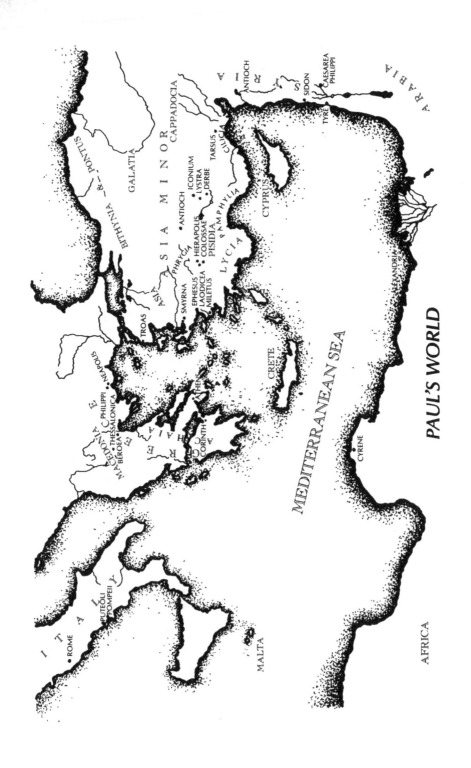

PAUL'S WORLD

convictions, his plans, and to spend time in prayer. How long this period of retreat was, we do not know. However, when it was over, he returned to Damascus and began to preach in the local synagogues that Jesus was the Son of God. You can imagine how people lifted their eyebrows! This was the man who a short time before was utilizing all his energy against the Christians. Some of the local Jews did not like this turn of events and plotted to kill him. With the help of friends he managed to escape from Damascus by being lowered from the city wall in a basket.

He came to Jerusalem but landed in a hornets' nest of suspicion. This should have been a surprise to no one. Not so long before he had been dragging Christians out of their homes. Was this some trick to win their confidence? Barnabas, a leader in the Jerusalem church, introduced him to the apostles, told them of Saul's experience of Jesus and of his preaching in Damascus, and convinced them of his sincerity. Having won acceptance among the Jerusalem Christians, he stayed with them a few days and preached "boldly in the name of the Lord." From there he went back to his hometown of Tarsus, laboring in behalf of the gospel for some six years. At the end of that time, Barnabas visited Saul and persuaded him to help him with the infant church in Antioch. Together they worked there about a year. Following this, about A.D. 45, Saul, who is henceforth referred to by Luke as Paul, began his first missionary journey in company with Barnabas. John Mark, Barnabas' cousin, started out with them but after a while left their company. This became the first of four famous missionary journeys undertaken by Paul.

PAUL'S MISSIONARY JOURNEYS

The first journey took him to the island of Cyprus where he converted the Roman proconsul. This was a good start. From there Paul and Barnabas headed north to Asia Minor and visited the towns of Perga, Antioch of Pisidia, Iconium, Lystra, and Derbe. In each place, the situation was almost the same. Paul preached to the gentiles who in turn warmed to his message. Then the local Jews, zealous for the Law of their faith, came on the scene and turned the people against him. Twice he escaped unharmed, but when he came to Lystra he was not so lucky. First the people treated Paul and Barnabas as gods, because Paul had healed a cripple. But when the troublesome Jews from Antioch and Iconium showed up, the tide quickly turned. They took hold of Paul, dragged him outside the city, stoned him, and left him for dead. When the crowd dispersed, his disciples came and ministered to him. His recovery was speedy. The next day he was on his way again. This first journey lasted about a year and a half.

Not long after they returned to Antioch, Paul and Barnabas were compelled to go to Jerusalem and face the council of the apostles there.

The subject dealt with receiving gentiles into the church. The question was: Could gentiles be taken into the church without first being required to undergo circumcision and keep the Law of Moses? This was debated hot and furiously by the council. At last the decision was made. Gentile Christians did not have to keep the Jewish Law to become Christians. Of course Paul was on the side of that decision, since that was the way he had been conducting his ministry to the gentiles. He did not demand their acceptance of the Jewish faith or practices. Rather he preached the gospel of a crucified and resurrected Christ who offered forgiveness of sins to all.

His second missionary journey took him again to Asia Minor, then over to Macedonia, to the town of Philippi. Here, together with his companion Silas, he was beaten and thrown into prison. Following his release he visited Thessalonica, Beroea, Athens, and Corinth, stopping at Ephesus in Asia Minor on the way home. His travels to Macedonia and Greece meant that for the first time the gospel was taken to Europe.

Paul's third missionary journey was spent mostly at Ephesus, where he worked for two years until he incurred the anger of a certain Demetrius, an image maker. At the end of the two years, he returned to Jerusalem even though he had been warned to stay away. There he was accused by the Jews of not observing the Law of Moses. An uproar followed. Things became so violent that Paul was arrested for disturbing the peace. The Jews tried to kill him, but the Roman authorities protected him. For safety's sake he was sent to Caesarea where he remained for two years waiting for his case to be tried. Finally he appealed to Caesar, and his request was granted. This meant he must be taken to Rome. As a Roman citizen, a privilege enjoyed by Paul through his father, he had the right of this appeal. After a hazardous journey by ship, Paul at long last reached the imperial city. He remained there for two years awaiting trial. At this point, the account in Acts ends. We do not know for certain what actually happend to Paul after this.

One thought is that he may have been tried and acquitted for lack of evidence. After his acquittal he may have traveled to Spain and other parts of the Mediterranean world. But it also seems likely that he was arrested again about A.D. 64 and most probably died at Rome under the terrible persecutions being waged by the insane emperor Nero.

PAUL: MINISTER OF A NEW COVENANT

Next to Jesus, Paul must go down as the greatest figure in the history of the Christian church. More than anyone else he was responsible for taking the infant Christian faith out of its Palestinian swaddling cloths and introducing it to the world. Paul has been called the apostle to the gentiles, and that he certainly was. He established new churches all over the empire in the face of almost impossible difficulties. Yet nothing deterred him from spreading the good news of a New Covenant—a covenant of the spirit, a covenant of freedom, a covenant of faith. What did he go through to spread this kind of good news? Read his own account of the difficulties encountered:

> Five times I have received at the hands of the Jews the forty lashes less one. Three times I have been beaten with rods; once I was stoned. Three times I have been shipwrecked; a night and a day I have been adrift at sea; on frequent journeys, in danger from rivers, danger from robbers, danger from my own people, danger from Gentiles, danger in the city, danger in the wilderness, danger at sea, danger from false brethren; in toil and hardship, through many a sleepless night, in hunger and thirst, often without food, in cold and exposure. And, apart from other things, there is the daily pressure upon me of my anxiety for all the churches.
> —2 Corinthians 11:24-28

In the face of all this, which would have crumpled a weaker man into the dust, he could say, "I count everything as loss because of the surpassing worth of knowing Christ Jesus my Lord [Phil. 3:8]."

PAUL'S LETTERS

Paul wrote letters to the churches he was instrumental in organizing. They were written to deal with certain situations that had arisen. These letters tell us a great deal about this man. The letters that seem to be most truly from his hand are Romans, 1 and 2 Corinthians, Galatians, Philippians, Colossians, 1 and 2 Thessalonians, and Philemon. These reveal the great faith of Paul and his insistence that a Christian is one who must live life by faith in the goodness of God. He constantly urged his readers to live their lives on a spiritual plane and to concern themselves for those values that do not pass away. He reminded them that when they were "in Christ," they were new persons, a "new creation." He told his readers repeatedly of the responsibilities of Christians in the New Covenant community, the church.

We can close the curtain on the drama of Paul's life with the following high note by one who was intimately acquainted with almost constant struggle and suffering:

> Who shall separate us from the love of Christ? Shall tribulation, or distress, or persecution, or famine, or nakedness, or peril, or sword? As it is written,
> "For thy sake we are being killed all the day long;
> we are regarded as sheep to be slaughtered."
> No, in all these things we are more than conquerors through him who loved us. For I am sure that neither death, nor life, nor angels, nor principalities, nor things present, nor things to come, nor powers,

163

nor height, nor depth, nor anything else in all creation, will be able to separate us from the love of God in Christ Jesus our Lord.

—Romans 8:35-39

In another letter Paul referred to himself as the minister of a new covenant. He was. His was the life that carried the covenant out into the larger world. He was the chief agent in this propulsion. However, after him came others. Ministers of the New Covenant have not ceased to carry it into new places through the centuries, including into our own day. And by God's grace the New Covenant will extend into an even more glorious future.

Epilogue:
THE KINGDOM OF GOD AND ETERNAL LIFE

God is the God of history. But God also reigns on the further side of history. God is the one who is the same yesterday, today, and forever. God is the Eternal One for whom a thousand years are but a sleep when it is past. This Eternal One sent Jesus Christ as the forger of the New Covenant. Within this covenant persons find joy and peace and meaning and purpose and forgiveness and eternal life. Not only is life redeemed for people here and now, this life is everlasting.

Here persons are but pilgrims, walking for a few short years upon the earth. Here there is no permanent abiding place, no real home. Here we have a place of testing and witness while we await expectantly the kingdom that already is. For the kingdom of God is not only the rule of God in the hearts of persons and the sovereignty of God over society. The kingdom of God is that eternal realm where God reigns supreme. It is this that we hold before our eyes as our hope while we live on the earth.

Paul had some things to tell us about the life beyond this life in 1 Corinthians 15. This great chapter stands as an epilogue, a resounding "amen" to the drama of the covenant. Our covenant story began with a prologue in which the stage was set by the telling of the story of Adam. Adam symbolizes all of us who turn our backs on the Creator, the Giver of life. What is our basic sin? It is our desire to be our own god and to ignore the God who created us. This way can lead only to ruin, to separation from God, and to death. But a new being has come, even Jesus Christ. His will was to do the will of God. For those who believe in Jesus, God's will is their will too. This way leads to redemption, fellowship, and life. Paul puts it this way:

> But in fact Christ has been raised from the dead, the first fruits of those who have fallen asleep. For as by a man came death, by a man has come also the resurrection of the dead. For as in Adam all die, so also in Christ shall all be made alive.
>
> The first man was from the earth, a man of dust; the second man is from heaven. As was the man of dust, so are those who are of the dust;

and as is the man of heaven, so are those who are of heaven. Just as we
have borne the image of the man of dust, we shall also bear the image
of the man of heaven. I tell you this, brethren: flesh and blood cannot
inherit the kingdom of God, nor does the perishable inherit the
imperishable.

—1 Corinthians 15:20-22, 47-50

When Paul speaks of our bearing "the image of the man of heaven," he
is of course referring to Jesus. What he is saying is this. Those who are
children of the New Covenant have the stamp of Jesus upon them, upon
their lives. They are not just a physical lump with a destiny that goes no
farther than the satisfaction of the senses. They are spiritual beings who
have an eternal destiny. God's love that has come to them in Jesus is not
just meant to make them happy for a few short years upon the earth. God's
love is meant to hold them eternally. How do we know this? Christ has
been raised from the dead. Because he lives so shall we. This is the
promise of the covenant, this is the great fact of the covenant. Paul rises to
a crescendo of joy as he ponders his most wonderful thought:

When the perishable puts on the imperishable, and the mortal puts
on immortality, then shall come to pass the saying that is written:
 "Death is swallowed up in victory."
 "O death, where is thy victory?
 O death, where is thy sting?"
The sting of death is sin, and the power of sin is the law. But thanks
be to God, who gives us the victory through our Lord Jesus Christ.

—1 Corinthians 15:54-57

The last book of the Bible, the book of Revelation, portrays this hope
somewhat differently. An apocalyptic book, it was originally written to
give hope and comfort and courage to early Christians who faced the
threat of death at the hands of Domitian, the Roman emperor. It was
written by a man named John, a Syrian Christian, about A.D. 93. It is
filled with the symbolism and imagery which is peculiar to such apocalyptic writings. This symbolism had a world of meaning to the Christians of
the first century, and there are ideas within this book that speak power-
fully to every age. This is particularly true of those ideas that have to do
with the time to come, which no one can describe, except in the language
of word picture and symbol. Perhaps there is no better way to bring down
the curtain on this presentation of the biblical drama than to share two of
these ideas. As John peered into the time that lies beyond, his thoughts
took this form:

Then I saw a new heaven and a new earth; for the first heaven and the
first earth had passed away, and the sea was no more. And I saw the
holy city, new Jerusalem, coming down out of heaven from God,

prepared as a bride adorned for her husband; and I heard a loud voice from the throne saying, "Behold, the dwelling of God is with men. He will dwell with them, and they shall be his people, and God himself will be with them; he will wipe away every tear from their eyes, and death shall be no more, neither shall there be mourning nor crying nor pain any more, for the former things have passed away."

—Revelation 21:14

And is it not of the very essence of the covenant when John says: "Behold, I stand at the door and knock; if any one hears my voice and opens the door, I will come in to him and eat with him, and he with me [Rev. 3:20]."

The covenant is a golden cord that runs through the Bible from beginning to end. It is the cord that binds people to their God and to one another. May it be such a cord for you.

Made in the USA
Las Vegas, NV
26 October 2021